Congressional Research Service

Funding for the Older Americans Act and Other Aging Services Programs

Angela Napili
Information Research Specialist

Kirsten J. Colello
Specialist in Health and Aging Policy

February 22, 2013

Congressional Research Service

7-5700

www.crs.gov

RL33880

CRS Report for Congress

Prepared for Members and Committees of Congress

Summary

The Older Americans Act (OAA) is the major federal vehicle for the delivery of social and nutrition services for older persons. These include supportive services, congregate nutrition services (meals served at group sites such as senior centers, schools, churches, or senior housing complexes), home-delivered nutrition services, family caregiver support, community service employment, the long-term care ombudsman program, and services to prevent the abuse, neglect, and exploitation of older persons. The OAA also supports grants to older Native Americans and research, training, and demonstration activities. The Administration on Aging (AOA) in the newly established Administration for Community Living (ACL), within the U.S. Department of Health and Human Services (HHS) administers most OAA programs. The exception is the Community Service Employment for Older Americans (CSEOA) program, which is administered by the U.S. Department of Labor (DOL). The ACL also administers several aging services programs authorized under the Public Health Service Act, such as the Alzheimer's Disease Supportive Services Program and the Lifespan Respite Care Program. Funding for OAA programs and other aging services is provided through appropriations legislation for the Departments of Labor, Health and Human Services, and Education, and Related Agencies (Labor-HHS-Education).

FY2012 funding for OAA programs totals $1.913 billion, 1% less than in FY2011. The President's FY2013 budget request proposes $1.907 billion for OAA programs, 0.3% less than the FY2012 level. The President's budget proposal would eliminate $6.5 million in discretionary OAA funding for Aging and Disability Resource Centers (ADRCs) also funded by the Patient Protection and Affordable Care Act (P.L. 111-148, as amended). The Continuing Appropriations Resolution, 2013 (CR; P.L. 112-175) became law on September 28, 2012. For most discretionary programs, including OAA programs, the CR continues funding at close to FY2012 levels. The CR provides funding for October 1, 2012, through March 27, 2013, although amounts may change depending on whether certain actions, such as sequestration, are taken pursuant to the Budget Control Act (P.L. 112-25) and the American Taxpayer Relief Act of 2012 (ATRA, P.L. 112-240).

Since the enactment of OAA, Congress has reauthorized and amended the act numerous times. In the past, OAA reauthorization has included extending the act's authorization of appropriations for a five-year period. The last OAA reauthorization occurred in 2006, when Congress enacted the Older Americans Act Amendments of 2006 (P.L. 109-365), which extended the act's authorization of appropriations for FY2007 through FY2011. The authorization of appropriations for most OAA programs expired at the end of FY2011. However, Congress has continued to appropriate funding for OAA authorized activities. In the 112th Congress, comprehensive OAA reauthorization legislation was introduced which would extend the authorization of appropriations for most OAA programs through FY2017 and would make various amendments to existing OAA authorities.

This report provides details of FY2011, FY2012, and FY2013 funding for OAA authorized activities, as well as for other aging services programs administered by ACL under other statutory authorities.

Contents

Figures

Tables

Appendixes

Contacts

Introduction

Originally enacted in 1965, the Older Americans Act (OAA) supports a wide range of social services and programs for older persons.[1] These include supportive services, congregate nutrition services (meals served at group sites such as senior centers, community centers, schools, churches, or senior housing complexes), home-delivered nutrition services, family caregiver support, community service employment, the long-term care ombudsman program, and services to prevent the abuse, neglect, and exploitation of older persons. Except for Title V, Community Service Employment for Older Americans (CSEOA), all programs are administered by the Administration on Aging (AOA) in the Administration for Community Living (ACL) within the Department of Health and Human Services (HHS).[2] Title V is administered by the Department of Labor's (DOL's) Employment and Training Administration.

The ACL also administers several aging services programs with funding authorized under non-OAA statutes.[3] This includes two programs authorized under the Public Health Service Act (PHSA): the Alzheimer's Disease Supportive Services Program and the Lifespan Respite Care Program. ACL administers the Chronic Disease Self-Management Program, the Elder Abuse Prevention Intervention program, and certain activities to implement the National Plan to Address Alzheimer's Disease, which are funded through the Prevention and Public Health Fund established by the Patient Protection and Affordable Care Act (ACA; P.L. 111-148, as amended). ACL also administers the National Clearinghouse for Long-Term Care Information, which is funded through the Deficit Reduction Act (DRA; P.L. 109-171, as amended). Discretionary funding for OAA programs and other ACL administered programs is provided through appropriations legislation for the Departments of Labor, Health and Human Services, and Education, and Related Agencies (Labor-HHS-Education). Funds for ACL programs (Titles II, III, IV, VI, and VII) are part of the HHS appropriations; Title V is part of the DOL appropriations.

Since the enactment of OAA, Congress has reauthorized and amended the act numerous times. In the past, OAA reauthorization has included extending the act's authorization of appropriations for a five-year period. The last OAA reauthorization occurred in 2006, when Congress enacted the Older Americans Act Amendments of 2006 (P.L. 109-365), which extended the act's authorization of appropriations for FY2007 through FY2011. While the authorization of appropriations under the act expired at the end of FY2011, Congress has continued to appropriate funding for OAA authorized activities for FY2012.

---

[1] The OAA statute defines "older individual" as someone aged 60 years or older. The Older Americans Act Amendments of 2006 (P.L. 109-365) extended the authorization of appropriations for OAA programs through FY2011. For further information, see CRS Report RL31336, *The Older Americans Act: Programs, Funding, and 2006 Reauthorization (P.L. 109-365)*, by Carol O'Shaughnessy and Angela Napili. An unofficial compilation of the OAA, as amended, is at the Administration on Aging (AOA) website, at http://www.aoa.gov/AoARoot/AoA_Programs/OAA.

[2] On April 16, 2012, HHS Secretary Sebelius announced the creation of the Administration for Community Living (ACL) which brings together the Administration on Aging, the Office of Disability, and the Administration on Developmental Disabilities (renamed the Administration on Intellectual and Developmental Disabilities) into one agency, http://www.hhs.gov/news/press/2012pres/04/20120416a.html. For more information on the ACL, see http://www.acl.gov.

[3] ACL also administers programs for persons with disabilities, such as programs under the Developmental Disabilities Assistance and Bill of Rights Act (DD Act). However, this report focuses on programs targeted to the older population and programs historically administered by AOA.

In the 112th Congress, the Senate Health, Education, Labor, and Pensions (HELP) Subcommittee on Primary Health and Aging and the Senate Special Committee on Aging separately held hearings on OAA reauthorization.[4] A comprehensive OAA reauthorization bill was also introduced in the 112th Congress; S. 2037 was introduced January 26, 2012 by Senator Sanders and entitled, "Older Americans Act Amendments of 2012." A similar bill, S. 3562 (introduced September 19, 2012 and also sponsored by Senator Sanders), includes additional provisions to reauthorize OAA. These reauthorization bills would have extended the authorization of appropriations for most OAA programs through FY2017 and would have made various amendments to existing OAA authorities.[5]

This report provides details of FY2011 and FY2012 funding for OAA, the President's FY2013 budget request, and the Continuing Appropriations Resolution, 2013 (CR; P.L. 112-175). It then discusses current and proposed funding for other programs administered by AOA, but authorized under other statutes. The appendixes provide more detailed funding information and history. **Table A-1** of **Appendix A** provides funding levels for OAA and other ACL aging services programs for FY2011 and FY2012, the President's FY2013 budget request, and the CR. **Table B-1** of **Appendix B** provides funding levels for OAA programs and other ACL aging services programs from FY2004 through FY2012. **Appendix C** shows the authorization of appropriations for each title of the act as stipulated by the 2006 Older Americans Act Amendments (P.L. 109-365).

For general background on DOL and HHS appropriations, see CRS Report R42588, *Labor, Health and Human Services, and Education: FY2013 Appropriations Overview*, coordinated by Karen E. Lynch; CRS Report R42010, *Labor, Health and Human Services, and Education: FY2012 Appropriations*, coordinated by Karen E. Lynch; and CRS Report R41521, *Labor, Health and Human Services, and Education: FY2011 Appropriations*, coordinated by Pamela W. Smith. For information on HHS funding for Public Health Service Agencies, see CRS Report R41737, *Public Health Service (PHS) Agencies: Overview and Funding, FY2010-FY2012*, coordinated by C. Stephen Redhead and Pamela W. Smith.

---

[4] U.S. Congress, Senate Committee on Health, Education, Labor, and Pensions, Subcommittee on Primary Health and Aging, *Senior Hunger and the Older Americans Act*, 112th Cong., 1st sess., June 21, 2011, http://help.senate.gov/hearings/hearing/?id=8dd4f284-5056-9502-5d30-a66996ae4d55. U.S. Congress, Senate Special Committee on Aging, *Meals, Rides, and Caregivers: What Makes the Older Americans Act so Vital to America's Seniors?*, 112th Cong., 1st sess., May 26, 2011, S. Hrg. 112-106 (Washington: GPO, 2011), http://www.gpo.gov/fdsys/pkg/CHRG-112shrg68180/pdf/CHRG-112shrg68180.pdf. U.S. Congress, Senate Special Committee on Aging, *Protecting the Promise to Our Seniors: Preserving Senior Programs*, 112th Cong., 1st sess., April 27, 2011, S. Hrg. 112-93 (Washington: GPO, 2011), http://www.gpo.gov/fdsys/pkg/CHRG-112shrg67864/pdf/CHRG-112shrg67864.pdf.

[5] The committees of jurisdiction for the OAA are the Senate Health, Education, Labor, and Pensions (HELP) Committee, Subcommittee on Primary Health and Aging, and the House Education and the Workforce Committee, Subcommittee on Higher Education and Workforce Training. Several other bills were also introduced in the 112th Congress to amend the OAA. These included H.R. 2786, Holocaust Survivors Assistance Act of 2011; H.R. 3610, Streamlining Workforce Development Programs Act of 2011; H.R. 4297, Workforce Investment Improvement Act of 2012; H.R. 3749, Expanding Opportunities for Older Americans Act of 2011; H.R. 6543, Care Coordination for Older Americans Act of 2012; S. 1744, Guardian Accountability and Senior Protection Act; S. 1750, Home Care Consumer Bill of Rights Act; S. 1819, Strengthening Services for America's Seniors Act; S. 1982, Improving Care for Vulnerable Older Citizens through Workforce Advancement Act of 2011; S. 2077, Elder Protection and Abuse Prevention Act; S. 3226, Americans Giving care to Elders (AGE) Act of 2012; S. 3358, Responding to Urgent needs of Survivors of the Holocaust Act; S. 3465, Care Coordination for Older Americans Act of 2012; S. 3575, LGBT Elder Americans Act of 2012; S. 3592, Locally Grown Foods for Older Americans Act; S. 3593, Improving Services and Activities for Diverse Elders Act; S. 3619, Streamlining Services for Older Veterans Act; and S. 3621, Seniors' Financial Bill of Rights Act.

Budget Overview

The following provides a brief overview of FY2012 funding for programs authorized by OAA, and other aging services programs that are administered by ACL but receive funding under non-OAA authorities. Next, this section briefly summarizes OAA and aging services programs provisions in the President's FY2013 budget and legislative activity in the 112th Congress, including the FY2013 Continuing Appropriations Resolution (CR; P.L. 112-175). Sequestration under the Budget Control Act (BCA; P.L. 112-25) and the American Taxpayer Relief Act of 2012 (ATRA; P.L. 112-240), as it relates to these programs, is also briefly described. For further information on funding levels for FY2011, FY2012, the President's FY2013 budget request, and the CR, see **Table A-1** in **Appendix A**.

FY2012 Funding

P.L. 112-74, the Consolidated Appropriations Act, 2012, was signed by President Obama on December 23, 2011.[6] The act provided $1.913 billion for OAA programs, 1% less than the FY2011 funding level of $1.932 billion. Funding levels for most OAA programs remained near FY2011 levels. Division F, Section 527 of the act applied a 0.189% across-the-board rescission to most Labor-HHS-Education items, including OAA and most aging services programs now administered by ACL. However, no funds were provided for Program Innovations, a reduction of $19.1 million in total funding from FY2011. Program Innovations funding has historically been used to test and demonstrate new approaches and best practices in aging services. Funding for AOA's Program Administration activities increased by $3.1 million to $23.1 million for FY2012. Funding for Alzheimer's Disease Supportive Services was reduced by $7.4 million (65%) to $4.0 million for FY2012.

Figure 1 shows the distribution of FY2012 OAA funding by title, with program level detail for Title III. Title III State and Community Programs on Aging received the largest proportion of OAA funding with 71.0% of funding appropriated to nutrition, supportive services, family caregivers, and health promotion activities. Almost one-fourth of OAA funding (23.4%) was allocated to Title V, the CSEOA Program. The remainder was allocated to AOA-administered activities under Title II (2.3%) and Title IV (0.4%), grants to Native Americans under Title VI (1.8%), and vulnerable elder rights protection activities under Title VII (1.1%).

FY2012 funding for other ACL-administered aging services programs (not shown) included $4.0 million for the Alzheimer's Disease Supportive Services Program and just under $2.5 million for the Lifespan Respite Care Program, both authorized under the PHSA. ACL also administers the Chronic Disease Self-Management Program, which received $10.0 million in FY2012 through the Prevention and Public Health Fund (PPHF) established by the ACA. Another $4.0 million from the PPHF was allocated to ACL for Alzheimer's Disease Prevention Education and Outreach in FY2012. An additional $6.0 million from the PPHF was allocated to ACL to test

---

[6] Prior to P.L. 112-74, funding for FY2012 was provided through a series of three continuing resolutions. P.L. 112-33, the Continuing Appropriations Act, 2012, provided funding through October 4, 2011. P.L. 112-36, the Continuing Appropriations Act, 2012, provided funding through November 18, 2011. P.L. 112-55, the Consolidated and Further Continuing Appropriations Act, 2012, provided funding through December 16, 2011. For most federal programs, including OAA and AOA programs, these continuing resolutions continued funding under the same authority and conditions as for FY2011, but with a 1.503% across-the-board reduction in the rate of operations.

---

elder abuse prevention interventions.[7] ACL also administers the National Clearinghouse for Long-Term Care Information, which received $3.0 million in FY2012 through mandatory DRA funds.

Figure 1. Older Americans Act, FY2012 Funding

(as a percentage of total OAA funding, $1.913 billion)

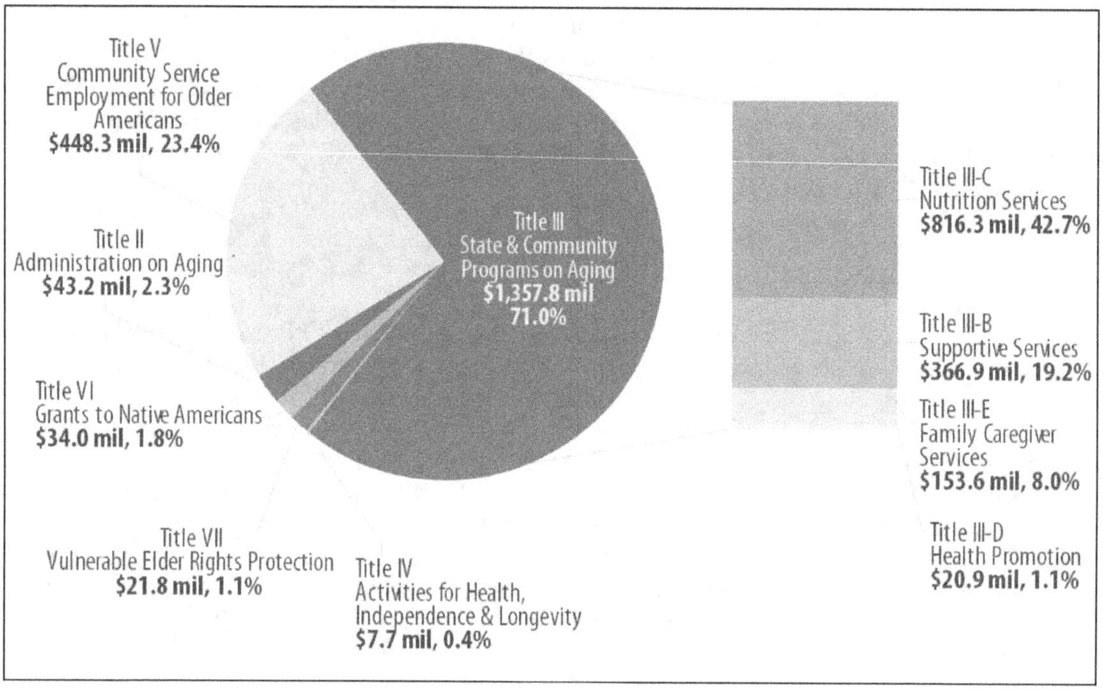

Title V
Community Service
Employment for Older
Americans
$448.3 mil, 23.4%

Title II
Administration on Aging
$43.2 mil, 2.3%

Title VI
Grants to Native Americans
$34.0 mil, 1.8%

Title III
State & Community
Programs on Aging
**$1,357.8 mil
71.0%**

Title VII
Vulnerable Elder Rights Protection
$21.8 mil, 1.1%

Title IV
Activities for Health,
Independence & Longevity
$7.7 mil, 0.4%

Title III-C
Nutrition Services
$816.3 mil, 42.7%

Title III-B
Supportive Services
$366.9 mil, 19.2%

Title III-E
Family Caregiver
Services
$153.6 mil, 8.0%

Title III-D
Health Promotion
$20.9 mil, 1.1%

Source: HHS, AOA, **Fiscal Year 2013** *Justification of Estimates for Appropriations Committee,* February 13, 2012, http://aoa.gov/AoARoot/About/Budget/DOCS/FY_2013_AoA_CJ_Feb_2012.pdf; Personal communication with G. Steven Hagy, Director, Office of Budget and Finance, AOA, April 4, 2012.

Note: Sums may not total due to rounding. Does not include other programs administered by ACL such as the Lifespan Respite Care Program and the Alzheimer's Disease Supportive Services Program.

FY2013 Budget Highlights

On February 13, 2012, the President released the Administration's FY2013 budget request, which proposes $1.907 billion for OAA programs, 0.3% less than the FY2012 level. The reduction is primarily due to the proposed elimination of $6.5 million in discretionary OAA funding for Aging and Disability Resource Centers (ADRCs); ADRCs would continue to receive $10.0 million in annual mandatory funding through the ACA. The FY2013 budget request also proposes transferring the administration of the CSEOA program from DOL to AOA, as well as the administration of State Health Insurance and Assistance Programs (SHIPs) from the Centers for Medicare and Medicaid Services (CMS) to AOA.[8] The FY2012 President's Budget proposal similarly proposed transferring the administration of these programs to AOA, but the FY2012

---

[7] HHS, Prevention and Public Health Fund, FY 2012 Allocation of Funds, http://www.hhs.gov/open/recordsandreports/prevention/index.html.

[8] The FY2013 Budget was released in February 2012 and reflected HHS's organizational chart at the time, referring to AOA rather than to ACL.

Consolidated Appropriations Act did not enact these proposals. To help carry out the new National Plan to Address Alzheimer's Disease, the Obama Administration also proposes to transfer $14.7 million from PPHF to AOA in FY2013. This funding would be used for public education and outreach and to expand support for persons with Alzheimer's disease and their families.[9]

The FY2013 budget request proposes to partially restore funding for Alzheimer's Disease Supportive Services by $5.5 million, from $4.0 million in FY2012 to $9.5 million in FY2013. (In FY2011, Alzheimer's Disease Supportive Services had received $11.4 million). It further proposes $8.0 million in new funding for Adult Protective Services (APS) State Demonstrations, including $1 million under Title VII for research and demonstration programs to address elder abuse and related issues in tribal nations. The FY2013 budget request also proposes to increase funding for AOA program administration by $0.2 million (1%). All other OAA and AOA aging services programs would continue to be funded at FY2012 levels.

Figure 2 shows total appropriated funding for OAA programs for FY2001 through FY2012, and the FY2013 budget request. From FY2006 to FY2010, OAA funding increased steadily from $1.783 billion to $2.328 billion, an overall increase of 31% over this time period. The American Recovery and Reinvestment Act (ARRA; P.L. 111-5) provided an additional $220 million to OAA programs in FY2009. OAA funding for FY2010 included a one-time special appropriation of $225 million to serve low-income seniors affected by the recession. The FY2012 funding level for OAA is $1.913 billion, which is a 1.0% decrease from the FY2011 funding level, and just under the FY2008 funding level. The President's FY2013 budget request is for $1.907 billion, 0.3% less than the FY2012 funding level.

---

[9] Personal communication with Michael Bernier, HHS Budget Office, May 16, 2012; HHS, *National Plan to Address Alzheimer's Disease,* May 2012, http://aspe.hhs.gov/daltcp/napa/NatlPlan.pdf.

Figure 2. Total Funding for Older Americans Act Programs, FY2001-FY2012, and FY2013 Budget Request

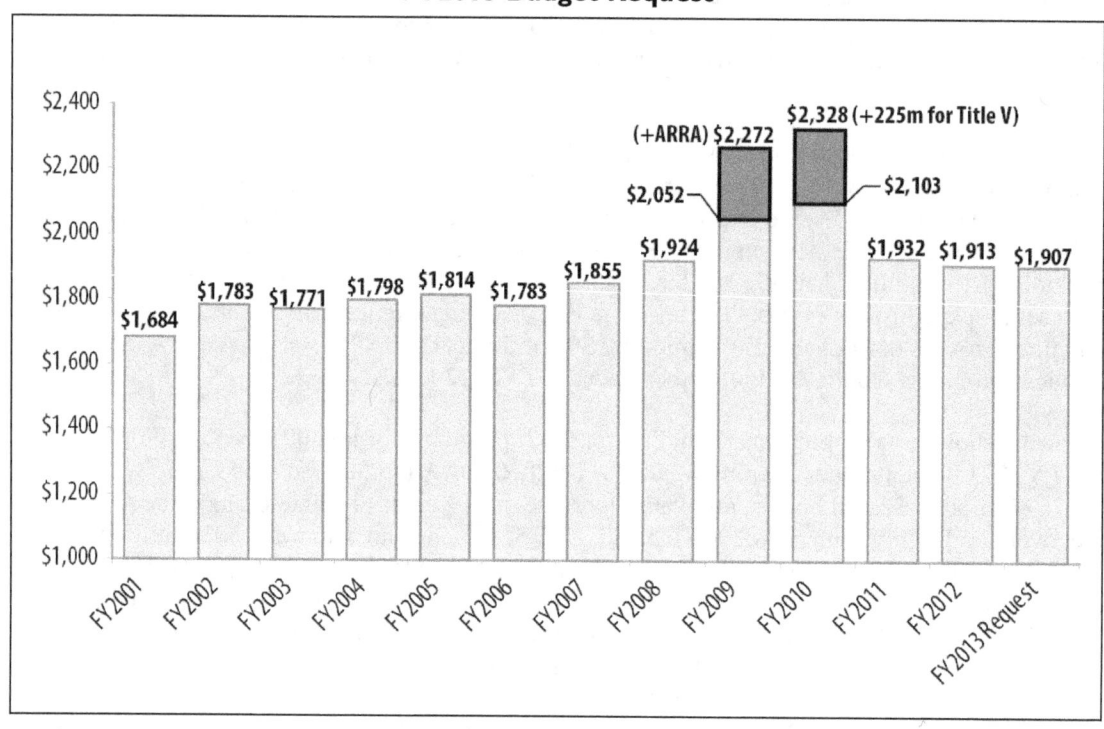

Source: Prepared by CRS based on appropriations legislation, committee reports, DOL, *Department of Labor, FY2011 Operating Plan,* http://www.dol.gov/dol/budget/2012/PDF/2011OperatingPlanTable.pdf; HHS, *The Department of Health and Human Services: FY 2011 Operating Plans;* and HHS, AOA, *Fiscal Year 2013 Justification of Estimates for Appropriations Committee,* February 13, 2012, http://aoa.gov/AoARoot/About/Budget/DOCS/ FY_2013_AoA_CJ_Feb_2012.pdf.

Note: ARRA = American Recovery and Reinvestment Act (P.L. 111-5).

Legislative Activity in the 112th Congress

The Senate Appropriations Committee reported its FY2013 Labor-HHS-Education Appropriations bill on June 14, 2012 (S. 3295). The accompanying committee report (S.Rept. 112-176) would appropriate funding for "Aging and Disability Services Programs" under the newly established ACL. Unlike the President's budget request, S. 3295 would maintain ADRC discretionary funding at FY2012 levels. S. 3295 would provide a total of $1.914 billion for OAA programs in FY2013, continuing total OAA program funding at similar levels compared with FY2012. It would also provide for the budget request's $8.0 million in new funding for APS State Demonstrations, including $1 million under Title VII for research and demonstration programs to address elder abuse and related issues in tribal nations. Furthermore, S. 3295 would transfer administration of SHIPs from CMS to ACL. This transfer was proposed in the President's FY2013 budget request.

On July 18, 2012, the House Appropriations Subcommittee on Labor, Health and Human Services, Education, and Related Agencies approved its draft FY2013 appropriations bill.[10] The

---

[10] S. Congress, House Committee on Appropriations, Subcommittee on Labor, Health and Human Services, Education, (continued...)

draft bill indicates that the reorganization establishing ACL would be ineffective for FY2013. According to the bill, in order for such reorganization to become effective in FY2014 the HHS Secretary would be required to follow a procedure described in the bill's accompanying House Appropriations Committee report. (However, to date no report has been produced as the draft bill has yet to be reported by the full House Appropriations Committee).

The House subcommittee's draft bill would provide $448.3 million for the CSEOA program under OAA Title V. It would also provide $1.440 billion total for AOA-administered OAA programs, the Alzheimer's Disease Supportive Services Program, the Lifespan Respite Care Program, and certain AOA-administered Medicare enrollment activities. (For comparison, FY2012 funding total for these activities was $1.471 billion).[11] No further action on the bill was taken by the House, either in the full House Appropriations Committee or in the House chamber.

FY2013 Continuing Resolution

The Continuing Appropriations Resolution, 2013 (CR; P.L. 112-175) became law on September 28, 2012. For most discretionary programs, including OAA programs, the CR continues funding at close to FY2012 levels for October 1, 2012 through March 27, 2013. The CR maintains annualized funding at the FY2012 levels provided by P.L. 112-74, plus an increase of 0.612% for most programs receiving discretionary appropriations. The CR also required federal agencies to submit to Congress an operating plan for funds provided by the CR and requires these plans to be updated in the event of sequestration or any extension of the CR itself.[12]

The HHS/ACL and DOL Operating Plans indicate that during the CR period, annualized funding for OAA programs will remain at $1.913 billion, similar to FY2012 levels. Although this report uses the amounts in the Operating Plans, these amounts are not final. There is uncertainty depending on whether certain actions, such as sequestration, are taken pursuant to the Budget Control Act (P.L. 112-25). Also, agencies may request additional funds from the 0.612% increase, and the HHS and DOL Secretaries have some authority to transfer funds among programs.

The Budget Control Act and FY2013 Sequestration

It is important to note that FY2013 discretionary appropriations are being considered in the context of the Budget Control Act of 2011 (BCA; P.L. 112-25) and the American Taxpayer Relief Act of 2012 (ATRA; P.L. 112-240). The BCA established discretionary spending limits for FY2012-FY2021. It also required that certain automatic across-the-board spending reductions,

---

(...continued)

and Related Agencies, *Making appropriations for the Departments of Labor, Health and Human Services, and Education, and related agencies for the fiscal year ending September 30, 2012, and for other purposes*, Draft bill, 112th Cong., 2nd sess., July 15, 2012, http://appropriations.house.gov/uploadedfiles/bills-112hr-sc-ap-fy13-laborhhsed.pdf.

[11] Consolidated Appropriations Act, 2012, P.L. 112-74, 125 Stat. 1079, 1115. The law provided $1.474 billion total for these activities, and Section 527 applied a rescission of 0.189%.

[12] P.L. 112-175, Sections 101, 106, and 116. ACL and DOL FY2013 Operating Plans are available from the authors upon request. The CR required that "only the most limited funding action of that permitted [by the CR] shall be taken in order to provide for continuation of projects and activities." The Office of Management and Budget (OMB) announced that during the CR period, the FY2012 base level of funding would be automatically apportioned to agencies and programs. However, the 0.612% increase would not be automatically apportioned; agencies would have to submit a written request to OMB to obtain these funds. Subsequently, the ACL and DOL Operating Plans for FY2013 do not reflect the 0.612% increase.

---

known as sequestration, would be triggered by the failure to enact deficit reduction legislation developed by the BCA-established Joint Select Committee on Deficit Reduction. Because Congress failed to enact such legislation by the BCA-specified deadline of January 15, 2012, sequestration was scheduled to take effect on January 2, 2013. However, the President signed ATRA on January 2, 2013, which postpones the proposed sequestration until March 1, 2013, and reduces the total (government-wide) sequestration amount by $24 billion. Unless Congress further amends or repeals the sequestration provisions in BCA and ATRA, automatic spending reductions are scheduled to take effect March 1, 2013.[13]

If sequestration is triggered, OMB is expected to determine the final sequestration amounts. On September 14, 2012, OMB released preliminary estimates of percentage reductions and dollar amount reductions for each account under the sequestration scheduled for January 2, 2013. OMB noted that "the estimates and classifications in the report are preliminary. If the sequestration were to occur, the actual results would differ based on changes in law and ongoing legal, budgetary, and technical analysis."[14]

To date, OMB's September 2012 estimates regarding spending reductions under sequestration have not been updated for recent changes in law, such as ATRA. According to the September 2012 OMB estimates, spending for the CSEOA program under OAA Title V would be reduced by 8.2%, or $37 million, from the FY2012 level. OMB did not provide estimates for other OAA programs per se. OMB did give an estimate for "Aging Services Programs," which include all non-Title V OAA programs, as well as several other programs administered by AOA. For Aging Services Programs, OMB estimated an FY2013 spending reduction of $122 million from the FY2012 level, including an 8.2% ($121 million) reduction in discretionary spending and a 7.6% ($1 million) reduction in mandatory spending.[15]

Older Americans Act Programs

The following provides details of FY2011 and FY2012 funding, FY2013 funding proposals, and FY2013 funding under the CR that runs through March 27, 2013, under OAA Titles II through VII. Title I (Declaration of Objectives) does not authorize appropriations. Each section includes a table of funding levels for FY2011 and FY2012, the FY2013 budget request, and the FY2013 CR (P.L. 112-175). The table is based on the FY2012 Consolidated Appropriations Act (P.L. 112-74/H.Rept. 112-331), ACL and DOL FY2013 Operating Plans, and email correspondence with ACL. Most tables include funding for specific activities within a larger budget line—in italicized font with appropriations amounts in parentheses. For further information on OAA program funding for these years, see **Table A-1** in **Appendix A**.

---

[13] For more background on sequestration, see CRS Report R42050, *Budget "Sequestration" and Selected Program Exemptions and Special Rules*, coordinated by Karen Spar.

[14] OMB, *OMB Report Pursuant to the Sequestration Transparency Act of 2012 (P.L. 112-155)*, September 14, 2012, pp. 3, 74 and 129, http://www.whitehouse.gov/sites/default/files/omb/assets/legislative_reports/stareport.pdf.

[15] Ibid.

Title II. Administration on Aging

Title II establishes AOA within HHS as the chief federal agency advocating for older persons and sets out the responsibilities of AOA and the Assistant Secretary for Aging. The Assistant Secretary is appointed by the President with the advice and consent of the Senate. Funding authorized under Title II goes toward program administration, the Senior Medicare Patrol program, ADRCs, and certain activities to support elder rights and the Aging Network. The Aging Network is made up of 56 State and Territorial Units on Aging (SUAs), 629 Area Agencies on Aging (AAAs), 256 tribal and Native Hawaiian organizations, and almost 20,000 aging and social service providers in local communities that provide OAA services.[16] Title II activities were funded at $43.2 million in FY2012, $3.1 million more than the FY2011 funding level of $40.1 million. Much of this difference was due to a $3.1 million increase in program administration funds for costs related to the expiration of the AOA headquarters' lease.

The FY2013 budget request proposes a total of $36.9 million for Title II activities, $6.3 million (15%) less than the FY2012 level. (See **Table 1**.) This decrease is due to the proposed elimination of $6.5 million in discretionary Title II funds for ADRCs. (ADRCs would continue to receive mandatory funds through ACA.) The FY2013 budget request also proposes to increase Title II program administration funding by $0.2 million. The CR maintains Title II funding at FY2012 levels. The following describes funding for Title II activities in greater detail: Program Administration, Senior Medicare Patrol, Aging Network Support Activities, Elder Rights Support Activities, and ADRCs.

**Table 1. Funding for Older Americans Act, Title II:
FY2011, FY2012, and FY2013 Budget Request and Continuing Resolution**

($ in millions)

	FY2011	FY2012	+/- FY2011	FY2013 Request	FY2013 CR
Title II: Administration on Aging	**$40.075**	**$43.160**	**+$3.085 +7.7%**	**$36.899**	**$43.160**
Program Administration	19.939	23.063	+3.124 +15.7%	23.259	23.063
Senior Medicare Patrolª	9.420	9.402	-0.018 -0.2%	9.402	9.402
Aging Network Support Activities (Title II portion)	2.891ᵇ	2.886	-0.006 -0.2%	2.886	2.886
National Eldercare Locator (non-add)	*(1.176)*	*(1.173)*	*(-0.003)* -0.2%	*(1.173)*	*(1.173)*
Pension Information and Counseling Program (non-add)	*(1.716)*	*(1.713)*	*(-0.003)* -0.2%	*(1.713)*	*(1.713)*
Elder Rights Support Activities (Title II portion)	1.355	1.352	-0.003 -0.2%	1.352	1.352

---

[16] HHS, AOA, *Fiscal Year 2013 Justification of Estimates for Appropriations Committee*, February 13, 2012, p. 9, http://aoa.gov/AoARoot/About/Budget/DOCS/FY_2013_AoA_CJ_Feb_2012.pdf.

	FY2011	FY2012	+/- FY2011	FY2013 Request	FY2013 CR
National Long-Term Care Ombudsman Resource Center (non-add)	(0.546)	(0.545)	(-0.001) -0.2%	(0.545)	(0.545)
National Center on Elder Abuse (non-add)	(0.809)	(0.807)	(-0.002) -0.2%	(0.807)	(0.807)
Aging and Disability Resource Centersᵇ	6.469	6.457	-0.012 -0.2%	0	6.457

Source: HHS, AOA, Fiscal Year 2013 Justification of Estimates for Appropriations Committee, February 13, 2012, http://aoa.gov/AoARoot/About/Budget/DOCS/FY_2013_AoA_CJ_Feb_2012.pdf; Personal communication with G. Steven Hagy, Director, Office of Budget and Finance, AOA, April 4, 2012; ACL, *Operating Plan for FY2013*, November, 2012.

Notes: FY2012 amounts reflect the 0.189% rescission required by P.L. 112-74, Division F, Section 527. The ACL Operating Plan for FY2013 does not break down funding by OAA program; CRS assumes that a program's funding level would remain the same as in FY2012. In AOA budget documents prior to FY2012, Aging Network Support Activities also included the National Long-Term Care Ombudsman Center, the National Center on Elder Abuse, Senior Medicare Patrol, and Health and Long-Term Care Programs (including ADRCs). Starting with FY2012, budget and appropriations documents list these programs in other categories. For comparability, this report reflects the categorizations in current budget and appropriations documents.

a. The Senior Medicare Patrol program is listed under Title II, for consistency with the AOA FY2013 Justification (pp. 36 and 145). Per personal communication with AOA, the Senior Medicare Patrol program receives funds under Title IV authority.

b. ADRC discretionary funding is listed under Title II, reflecting the Older Americans Act statute (§202(b)(8)) and for consistency with the AOA FY2013 Justification (p. 158). Per personal communication with AOA, ADRCs receive discretionary funds under Title IV authority.

Program Administration

For AOA program administration, the agency received $23.1 million in FY2012, $3.1 million more than the FY2011 level of $19.9 million. The final FY2012 funding level was close to the $23.1 million proposed in Senate FY2012 Labor-HHS-Education bill S. 1599/S.Rept. 112-84, which stated that "The Committee recommendation includes funding for tenant improvement and other costs related to the expiration of AoA's lease and a possible office relocation."[17] The FY2013 budget request proposes $23.3 million for AOA program administration, a $0.2 million (1%) increase over the FY2012 level. AOA states that this amount should support the same staffing levels as in FY2012, with additional funds used for the costs of the lease expiration and relocation of AOA headquarters which is expected in 2013.[18] The CR maintains AOA program administration funding at the FY2012 level.

Senior Medicare Patrol

The Senior Medicare Patrol Program funds projects that educate older Americans and their families to recognize and report Medicare and Medicaid fraud. Discretionary funding was $9.4

---

[17] S.Rept. 112-84, p. 153.

[18] HHS, AOA, *Fiscal Year 2013 Justification of Estimates for Appropriations Committees*, pp. 172-174. For ADRCs, Senior Medicare Patrol, the National Clearinghouse for Long-Term Care, and new programs that the FY2013 budget request proposes to assign to AOA (SHIPs, CSEOA, and the APS Demonstration Program), program administration funds are being requested separately as part of each program's respective request.

million in FY2011. For FY2012, the funding level was the same, minus the 0.189% across-the-board rescission required for most Labor-HHS-Education line items by the FY2012 Consolidated Appropriations Act. For FY2013, the budget request proposes to maintain discretionary funding at the FY2012 level. The CR also maintains discretionary funding at the FY2012 level. The Senior Medicare Patrol program also receives mandatory funding provided through Health Care Fraud and Abuse Control (HCFAC) funds, which are distributed to anti-fraud activities from the Medicare Trust Fund at the joint discretion of the HHS Secretary and Attorney General. HCFAC funding for the program was $3.3 million in FY2011 and $10.7 million in FY2012.

Aging Network Support Activities (Title II portion)

Funding provided under Title II goes toward certain authorized activities that support the Aging Network, including the following activities.

- *The National Eldercare Locator* assists individuals, through a nationwide toll-free phone number and website, in identifying community resources for older persons.[19]

- *The Pension Counseling and Information Program* provides funds to six regional counseling projects that help older Americans learn about and receive the retirement benefits to which they are entitled.

These Title II Aging Network Support activities received $2.9 million in FY2012, slightly less than FY2011 levels. The FY2013 budget request proposes to maintain funding at FY2012 levels. The CR also maintains Aging Network Support Activities funding at the FY2012 level.

Elder Rights Support Activities (Title II portion)

Elder Rights Support Activities authorized under Title II of the OAA include the following activities.

- *The National Center on Elder Abuse* provides information to the public and professionals regarding elder abuse prevention activities, and provides training and technical assistance to state elder abuse agencies and to community-based organizations.

- *The National Long-Term Care Ombudsman Resource Center* provides training and technical assistance to state and local long-term care ombudsmen.

Title II Elder Rights Support Activities received $1.4 million in FY2012, slightly less than FY2011 levels. The FY2013 budget request proposes to maintain funding at FY2012 levels. The CR also maintains Elder Rights Support Activities funding at the FY2012 level.

Aging and Disability Resource Centers

The aim of Aging and Disability Resource Centers (ADRCs) is to create "one-stop shop" single entry points for information about the range of public and private long-term services and supports (LTSS) available to consumers. ADRCs may provide services such as information and referral to

---

[19] The National Eldercare Locator can be reached through http://www.eldercare.gov or 1-800-677-1116.

public and private LTSS, offer options counseling, and provide eligibility determinations for public programs such as Medicaid. ADRCs also help "create formal collaborations" among hospitals, nursing homes, and community agencies and organizations to assist individuals as they move among different care settings. There are currently more than 300 ADRC sites nationwide, operating in 50 states, 3 territories, and the District of Columbia.[20]

Discretionary funding to ADRCs was $6.5 million in FY2011. The FY2012 funding level was the same, minus the 0.189% across-the-board rescission required for most Labor-HHS-Education line items by the FY2012 Consolidated Appropriations Act. In addition, ACA Section 2405 provided mandatory appropriations for ADRCs at $10.0 million for each year from FY2010 to FY2014. Thus, for FY2011 and FY2012, the total annual ADRC funding was $16.5 million. For FY2013, the budget request proposes no discretionary funding for ADRCs; ADRCs would continue to receive mandatory funds from ACA ($10.0 million in FY2013). The CR maintains ADRC discretionary funding at the FY2012 level.

Title III. Grants for State and Community Programs on Aging

The major program under the OAA, Title III—Grants for State and Community Programs on Aging—authorizes grants to 56 SUAs and 629 AAAs to act as advocates on behalf of, and to coordinate programs for, older persons.[21] Title III accounted for 71% of the OAA's total FY2012 funding ($1.358 billion out of $1.913 billion). (See **Table 2**.) States receive separate allotments of funds for supportive services and centers, family caregiver support, congregate nutrition, home-delivered nutrition, the nutrition services incentive grant program, and disease prevention and health promotion services.[22] The OAA allows states some flexibility to transfer funds among Title III programs. For example, in FY2010, states collectively transferred a net total of $82.6 million from congregate nutrition to supportive services and home-delivered nutrition.[23]

Title III services are available to all persons aged 60 and older, but are targeted at those with the greatest economic or social need, particularly low-income and minority persons and older persons residing in rural areas. In FY2010, the most recent year for which data are available, 10.8 million older persons were served by Title III programs.[24] Means testing is prohibited. Participants are encouraged to make voluntary contributions for services they receive. States are allowed to implement cost-sharing policies for certain services on a sliding fee scale basis, but older persons

---

[20] HHS, AOA, *Fiscal Year 2013 Justification of Estimates for Appropriations Committees*, pp. 158-164. A directory of ADRCs is at the Aging and Disability Resource Center Technical Assistance Exchange website at http://www.adrc-tae.org/tiki-index.php?page=ADRCLocator.

[21] The 56 State Units on Aging include units in 50 states, 5 U.S. territories, and the District of Columbia. More information is at the AOA website at http://www.aoa.gov/AoARoot/AoA_Programs/OAA/Aging_Network/Index.aspx and http://www.aoa.gov/AoARoot/AoA_Programs/OAA/.

[22] State allotments for Title III programs are listed at HHS, AOA, *Funding Allocations to State and Tribal Organizations*, http://www.aoa.gov/AoARoot/AoA_Programs/OAA/Aging_Network/State_Allocations/index.aspx. More background on Title III nutrition services is in CRS Report RS21202, *Older Americans Act: Title III Nutrition Services Program*, by Kirsten J. Colello.

[23] AOA, *FY 2010 Profile of State OAA Programs: United States*, Part I, at http://www.aoa.gov/aoaroot/program_results/spr/2010/profiles/us.xls.

[24] HHS, AOA, Aging Network, *Aging Integrated Database (AGID)*, 2010 State Program Reports, Total Counts: Clients Served - All Services: 50 States + DC & Territories, http://www.data.aoa.gov/.

---

must not be denied services due to failure to make cost-sharing payments. State, local, and private funding sources also supplement federal OAA funds for these services.[25]

In FY2010, Title III services included the provision of 145.5 million home-delivered meals; 96.4 million congregate meals; 26 million rides to medical appointments, grocery stores, and other activities; 35 million hours of personal care, homemaker, and chore services; 10 million hours of adult day care/adult day health services; and 5.9 million persons served through preventive health programs such as medication management and falls prevention.[26]

Table 2. Funding for Older Americans Act, Title III: FY2011, FY2012, and FY2013 Budget Request and Continuing Resolution

($ in millions)

	FY2011	FY2012	+/- FY2011	FY2013 Request	FY2013 CR
Title III: Grants for State and Community Programs on Aging	**$1,360.342**	**$1,357.772**	**-$2.570** **-0.2%**	**$1,357.772**	**$1,357.770**
Nutrition services	817.835	816.290	-1.545 -0.2%	816.290	816.289
Congregate meals (non-add)	*(439.901)*	*(439.070)*	*(-0.831)* *-0.2%*	*(439.070)*	*(439.070)*
Home-delivered meals (non-add)	*(217.241)*	*(216.831)*	*(-0.410)* *-0.2%*	*(216.831)*	*(216.830)*
Nutrition services incentive grants (non-add)	*(160.693)*	*(160.389)*	*(-0.304)* *-0.2%*	*(160.389)*	*(160.389)*
Supportive services and centers	367.611	366.916	-0.695 -0.2%	366.916	366.916
Family caregivers	153.912	153.621	-0.291 -0.2%	153.621	153.621
Disease prevention/health promotion	20.984	20.945	-0.039 -0.2%	20.945	20.944

Source: HHS, AOA, *Fiscal Year 2013 Justification of Estimates for Appropriations Committee*, February 13, 2012, http://aoa.gov/AoARoot/About/Budget/DOCS/FY_2013_AoA_CJ_Feb_2012.pdf; ACL, *Operating Plan for FY2013*, November, 2012.

Note: FY2012 amounts reflect the 0.189% rescission required by P.L. 112-74, Division F, Section 527.

Title III programs received $1.360 billion in FY2011. For FY2012, Title III programs were funded at $1.358 billion, which was the same as FY2011, less the 0.189% across-the-board rescission required for most Labor-HHS-Education line items under the FY2012 Consolidated Appropriations Act. The act also required that Title III disease prevention and health promotion funding be used only for activities demonstrated to be evidence-based and effective. For FY2013, the budget request proposes to maintain funding for Title III programs at FY2012 levels. The CR maintains Title III funding at close to the FY2012 level.

---

[25] HHS, AOA, *Fiscal Year 2013 Justification of Estimates for Appropriations Committees*, pp. 47, 55.

[26] Ibid., pp. 44-45, 56, 69.

Title IV. Activities for Health, Independence, and Longevity

Title IV of the OAA authorizes the Assistant Secretary for Aging to award funds for training, research, and demonstration projects in the field of aging.[27] Title IV programs include certain activities to support the Aging Network, certain activities to support elder rights, and Program Innovations. Title IV activities received $27.1 million in FY2011 and $7.7 million in FY2012, a $19.3 million (72%) decrease. Much of this difference was due to the elimination of funding for Program Innovations, which had received $19.1 million in FY2011. For FY2013, the budget request proposes Title IV funding of $7.7 million, which would maintain FY2012 funding levels. (See **Table 3.**) The CR maintains Title IV funding at FY2012 levels. The following describes funding for Title IV activities in greater detail: Aging Network Support Activities, Elder Rights Support Activities, and Program Innovations.

Table 3. Funding for Older Americans Act, Title IV: FY2011, FY2012, and FY2013 Budget Request and Continuing Resolution

($ in millions)

	FY2011	FY2012	+/- FY2011	FY2013 Request	FY2013 CR
Title IV: Activities for Health, Independence, and Longevity	**$27.102**	**$7.723**	**-$19.378 -71.5%**	**$7.723**	**$7.723**
Aging Network Support Activities (Title IV portion)	5.292	4.988	-0.305 -5.8%	4.988	4.988
National Alzheimer's Call Center (non-add)	*(0.998)*	*(0.998)*	*(0)*	*(0.998)*	*(0.998)*
National Education & Resource Center on Women & Retirement (non-add)	*(0.249)*	*(0.248)*	*(-0.001) -0.4%*	*(0.248)*	*(0.248)*
National Resource Centers on Native Americans (non-add)	*(0.692)*	*(0.691)*	*(-0.001) -0.1%*	*(0.691)*	*(0.691)*
National Minority Aging Organizations (non-add)	*(0.932)*	*(0.930)*	*(-0.002) -0.2%*	*(0.930)*	*(0.930)*
National Technical Assistance Resource Center for LGBT Elders (non-add)	*(0.300)*	*(0.299)*	*(-0.001) -0.2%*	*(0.299)*	*(0.299)*
Multigenerational Civic Engagement (non-add)	*(0.980)*	*(0.978)*	*(-0.002) -0.2%*	*(0.978)*	*(0.978)*
Program Performance and Technical Assistance (non-add)	*(1.142)*	*(0.843)*	*(-0.299) -26.2%*	*(0.843)*	*(0.843)*
Elder Rights Support Activities (Title IV portion)	2.741	2.736	-0.005 -0.2%	2.736	2.736
Model Approaches to Statewide Legal Systems (non-add)	*(1.996)*	*(1.992)*	*(-0.004) -0.2%*	*(1.992)*	*(1.992)*
National Legal Assistance and Support Projects (non-add)	*(0.745)*	*(0.744)*	*(-0.001) -0.1%*	*(0.744)*	*(0.744)*
Program Innovations	19.069	0	-19.069 -100%	0	0

---

[27] A compendium of many Title IV grant projects is at http://www.aoa.gov/AoARoot/Grants/Compendium/index.aspx.

	FY2011	FY2012	+/- FY2011	FY2013 Request	FY2013 CR
Health and Long-Term Care Programs, excluding *ADRCs (non-add)*	*(14.079)*	*(0)*	*(-14.079)* *-100%*	*(0)*	*(0)*
Community Innovations for Aging in Place (non-add)	*(4.990)*	*(0)*	*(-4.990)* *-100%*	*(0)*	*(0)*

Source: HHS, AOA, *Fiscal Year 2013 Justification of Estimates for Appropriations Committee,* February 13, 2012, http://aoa.gov/AoARoot/About/Budget/DOCS/FY_2013_AoA_CJ_Feb_2012.pdf; Personal communication with G. Steven Hagy, Director, Office of Budget and Finance, AOA, April 4, 2012; ACL, *Operating Plan for FY2013,* November, 2012.

Notes: FY2012 amounts reflect the 0.189% rescission required by P.L. 112-74, Division F, Section 527. The ACL Operating Plan for FY2013 does not break down funding by OAA program; CRS assumes that a program's funding level would remain the same as in FY2012. In AOA budget documents prior to FY2012, the categorization of Title IV activities was significantly different: Community Innovations for Aging in Place was under Aging Network Support Activities, and Program Innovations included all the Title IV items now listed under Aging Network Support Activities and Elder Rights Support Activities. For comparability, this report reflects the categorizations in FY2012 and FY2013 budget and appropriations documents.

Aging Network Support Activities (Title IV portion)

Funding provided under Title IV goes toward various activities that support the Aging Network, including the following activities.

- *The National Alzheimer's Call Center* is staffed by customer service workers and social workers; it provides free information, referrals, and counseling for persons with Alzheimer's disease, their families, and caregivers.

- *The National Education & Resource Center on Women & Retirement* provides workshops and information on financial education and retirement planning for women.

- *National Resource Centers on Native American Elders* provide research and technical information on health, long-term services and supports, elder abuse, mental health, and other issues relevant to older Native Americans.

- *National Minority Aging Organizations Technical Assistance Centers* provide culturally and linguistically appropriate information on health promotion and disease prevention for Asian-Pacific American, Native American, Hispanic, and African-American older individuals.

- *The National Technical Assistance Resource Center for LGBT Elders* aims to educate mainstream aging services organizations about issues related to lesbian, gay, bisexual, and transgender (LGBT) elders, to educate LGBT organizations about issues related to older adults, and to educate LGBT individuals about long-term care planning.

- *Multigenerational Civic Engagement* supports model programs in senior civic engagement and volunteer engagement.

- *Program Performance and Technical Assistance* supports the development of outcome measures and performance measurement tools to assess the results of OAA programs.

Funding for the above activities was $5.3 million in FY2011 and $5.0 million in FY2012, a $0.3 million (5.8%) decrease. Most of this decrease was due to a $0.3 million reduction in Program Performance and Technical Assistance funding. Prior to FY2012, all of the above programs were previously funded under the "Program Innovations" line item.[28] The FY2013 request proposes to maintain funding at FY2012 levels. The CR maintains Aging Network Support Activities funding at the FY2012 level.

Elder Rights Support Activities (Title IV portion)

Elder Rights Support Activities authorized under Title IV of the OAA include the following activities.

- *Model Approaches to Statewide Legal Assistance Systems* assists states to integrate senior legal helplines into broader state legal service delivery networks.

- *National Legal Assistance and Support Projects* provide services such as case consultation, training, technical assistance, and information dissemination for aging and legal services networks.

For FY2012, Title IV Elder Rights Support Activities received $2.7 million, slightly less than the FY2011 amount. The FY2013 budget request proposes to maintain funding at FY2012 levels. The CR maintains Elder Rights Support Activities funding at the FY2012 level.

Program Innovations

In the past, Program Innovations funding was intended to test and to demonstrate new approaches and best practices in aging services. The FY2012 Consolidated Appropriations Act provides no funding for Program Innovations, and no funds have been proposed in the FY2013 budget. The CR does not provide Program Innovations funding either. In FY2011, Program Innovations received $19.1 million for the following two programs.

- *Health and Long-Term Care Programs* included evidence-based disease prevention programs and nursing home diversion programs targeted to individuals at risk of Medicaid enrollment. (ADRCs were originally included in this initiative but now receive separate discretionary funding, see Title II. Administration on Aging.)

- The *Community Innovations for Aging in Place* program provided grants to help older individuals stay in their communities and to provide services to individuals in Naturally Occurring Retirement Communities (NORCs).

Program Innovations funding also supported the development of programs that are now funded through other budget items, such as ADRCs, Chronic Disease Self-Management Programs, Model Approaches to Statewide Legal Assistance Systems, National Legal Assistance and Support Projects, and many of the programs now being funded under Aging Network Support Activities. Program Innovations also provided funds for congressionally directed special projects, including projects related to wellness, falls prevention, caregiver services, elder abuse, and supportive

---

[28] HHS, *Department of Health and Human Services – FY2011 Operating Plans*, 2011.

services to older individuals in NORCs. Congressionally directed special projects received funding in FY2010 but not in FY2011 or FY2012.[29]

Title V. Community Service Employment for Older Americans

Title V, Community Service Employment for Older Americans (CSEOA), also known as the Senior Community Service Employment Program (SCSEP), has as its purpose the promotion of useful part-time opportunities in community service activities for unemployed low-income[30] persons who are 55 years or older and who have poor employment prospects. The Title V program is administered by DOL's Employment and Training Administration; it is the only OAA program not administered by AOA. For FY2012, Title V represented 23% of OAA funding ($448.3 million out of $1.913 billion). (See **Table 4**.)

CSEOA participants work part-time in a variety of community service jobs, such as in day care centers, libraries, schools, landscaping centers, and hospitals.[31] The program operates on a program year (PY) basis from July 1 through June 30.[32] For PY2011 (ending June 30, 2012), DOL estimates that CSEOA supported 46,309 job slots, serving about 85,113 participants, at a cost of $6,339 per participant.[33] Enrollees are paid no less than the highest of the federal minimum wage, the state or local minimum wage, or the prevailing wage paid by the same employer for similar public occupations. In addition to wages, enrollees receive training, physical examinations, personal and job-related counseling, transportation for employment purposes (under certain circumstances), and placement assistance into unsubsidized jobs. In PY2010, 47% of participants who exited the program found employment in the following quarter; of those, 70% remained employed through the next two quarters.[34]

The 2006 Older Americans Act Amendments (P.L. 109-365) maintained the program focus on employing older people in community service jobs and reemphasized the community service aspects of the program. While the program's purpose is to move participants into unsubsidized employment, the amendments recognized that many older people who have special needs may need to remain in subsidized employment and that the program supplements the income for some

---

[29] Congressionally directed funding totaled $5.974 million in FY2010; the funded projects were listed in H.Rept. 111-366, pp. 1041-1042.

[30] Participants' incomes must be no greater than 125% of the federal poverty guidelines. 20 C.F.R. §641.500.

[31] DOL, *SCSEP Frequently Asked Questions*, http://www.doleta.gov/Seniors/html_docs/docs/seniorsFAQ.cfm.

[32] Program Year 2012 allotments were announced in DOL, Employment and Training Administration, Program Year 2012 Planning Instructions and Allotments for Senior Community Service Employment Program (SCSEP) State and Territorial Grant Applicants, Training and Employment Guidance Letter No. 26-11, Washington, DC, April 30, 2012, http://wdr.doleta.gov/directives/corr_doc.cfm?DOCN=3261. Program Year 2011 allotments were announced in DOL, Employment and Training Administration, Program Year 2011 Planning Instructions and Allotments for SCSEP Grant Applicants, Training and Employment Guidance Letter No. 25-10, Washington, DC, May 10, 2011, http://wdr.doleta.gov/directives/corr_doc.cfm?docn=3020. Allotments for previous program years are posted at DOL, Training and Employment Guidance Letters, http://www.doleta.gov/Seniors/html_docs/TEGL.cfm.

[33] There are more participants than job slots in a given program year because as participants leave the program, their job slots can be filled by new participants. DOL, FY2013 *Congressional Budget Justification, Employment and Training Administration, Community Service Employment for Older Americans*, p. CSEOA-15, http://www.dol.gov/dol/budget/2013/PDF/CBJ-2013-V1-06.pdf.

[34] DOL, FY2013 *Congressional Budget Justification, Employment and Training Administration, Community Service Employment for Older Americans*, p. CSEOA-11.

---

workers who cannot find jobs in the private economy.[35] On September 1, 2010, DOL promulgated a final rule implementing changes made by the 2006 amendments.[36] These changes include a new 48-month limit on individual participation, increases in funds available for training and supportive services, and a requirement that national grants be recompeted every four years, among other changes. DOL conducted the competition for national grantees in FY2012.[37]

Table 4. Funding for Older Americans Act, Title V:
FY2011, FY2012, and FY2013 Budget Request and Continuing Resolution

($ in millions)

	FY2011	FY2012	+/- FY2011	FY2013 Request	FY2013 CR
Title V: Community Service Employment for Older Americans	$449.100	$448.251	-$0.849 -0.2%	$448.251	$448.251

Source: HHS, AOA, *Fiscal Year 2013 Justification of Estimates for Appropriations Committee*, February 13, 2012, http://aoa.gov/AoARoot/About/Budget/DOCS/FY_2013_AoA_CJ_Feb_2012.pdf; DOL, *Operating Plan for FY2013*, November, 2012.

Note: The FY2012 amount reflects the 0.189% rescission required by P.L. 112-74, Division F, Section 527.

For FY2012, CSEOA was funded at the same FY2011 level minus the 0.189% across-the-board rescission required for most Labor-HHS-Education line items by the FY2012 Consolidated Appropriations Act. The FY2013 budget request proposes to maintain funding at $448.3 million. It also proposes to transfer responsibility for administering the CSEOA program from DOL to AOA, arguing that participants would benefit from CSEOA's integration with other support programs administered by AOA and other safety net programs administered by HHS.[38] Of the 56 state and territorial grantees operating CSEOA programs, 17 are in state labor departments, whereas the rest are in aging, senior services, or health and human services departments. The budget request states that the transfer would consolidate federal OAA oversight under one department, "streamlining operations and putting federal administration of CSEOA in alignment with operations in the field." The proposal notes that AOA shares CSEOA's mission of "helping older Americans maintain their independence (both economic independence and living arrangements) and active participation in communities."[39] Current law does not allow for such a transfer through administrative action alone; Congress would have to pass legislation authorizing such a transfer to take effect.[40] The FY2012 President's Budget similarly proposed transferring CSEOA to AOA. The FY2012 Consolidated Appropriations Act did not enact this transfer. Under the CR, Title V funding remains at DOL and is maintained at the FY2012 level.

---

[35] For further information, see CRS Report RL31336, *The Older Americans Act: Programs, Funding, and 2006 Reauthorization (P.L. 109-365)*, by Carol O'Shaughnessy and Angela Napili.

[36] DOL, Employment and Training Administration, "Senior Community Service Employment Program; Final Rule," 75 *Federal Register* 53786, September 1, 2010. The rule's effective date was October 1, 2010.

[37] The grant announcement was posted at http://www.grants.gov/search/search.do?oppId=150653&mode=VIEW.

[38] HHS, AOA, *Fiscal Year 2013 Justification of Estimates for Appropriations Committees*, p. 76.

[39] Ibid. p. 76; DOL, *FY2013 Congressional Budget Justification, Employment and Training Administration, Community Service Employment for Older Americans*, pp. CSEOA-12 to CSEOA-13.

[40] The Administration proposed legislative language to effect the transfer in HHS, AOA, *Fiscal Year 2013 Justification of Estimates for Appropriations Committees*, pp. 26-27; and DOL, FY2013 *Congressional Budget Justification, Employment and Training Administration, Community Service Employment for Older Americans*, p. CSEOA-1.

Title VI. Grants for Services for Native Americans

Title VI authorizes funds for supportive and nutrition services to older Native Americans. Funds are awarded directly by AOA to Indian tribal organizations, Native Alaskan organizations, and non-profit groups representing Native Hawaiians. To be eligible for funding, a tribal organization must represent at least 50 Native American elders aged 60 and older. In FY2011, grants were awarded to 256 tribal organizations representing 400 Indian tribes, including two organizations serving Native Hawaiian elders.[41] The program provides services such as transportation, home-delivered and congregate nutrition services, information and referral, and a wide range of home care services. Title VI also authorizes caregiver support services to Native American elders. Respite, caregiver training, information and outreach, counseling, and support groups are among the services provided.

In FY2011, Title VI programs received $34.0 million. For FY2012, funding levels were the same, minus the 0.189% across-the-board rescission required for most Labor-HHS-Education line items by the FY2012 Consolidated Appropriations Act. For FY2013, the budget request proposes to maintain Title VI funding at the FY2012 level, and the CR similarly maintains funding at this level. (See **Table 5**.)

Table 5. Funding for Older Americans Act, Title VI: FY2011, FY2012, and FY2013 Budget Request and Continuing Resolution

($ in millions)

	FY2011	FY2012	+/- FY2011	FY2013 Request	FY2013 CR
Title VI: Grants to Native Americans	**$34.029**	**$33.965**	**-$0.064 -0.2%**	**$33.965**	**$33.965**
Supportive and nutrition services	27.653	27.601	-0.052 -0.2%	27.601	27.601
Native American family caregivers	6.376	6.364	-0.012 -0.2%	6.364	6.364

Source: HHS, AOA, *Fiscal Year 2013 Justification of Estimates for Appropriations Committee*, February 13, 2012, http://aoa.gov/AoARoot/About/Budget/DOCS/FY_2013_AoA_CJ_Feb_2012.pdf; ACL, *Operating Plan for FY2013*, November, 2012.

Note: FY2012 amounts reflect the 0.189% rescission required by P.L. 112-74, Division F, Section 527.

Title VII. Vulnerable Elder Rights Protection Activities

Title VII authorizes the Long-Term Care (LTC) Ombudsman Program as well as Elder Abuse, Neglect, and Exploitation Prevention Programs. Most Title VII funding is directed at the LTC Ombudsman Program. Of the $21.8 million in FY2012, more than three-quarters ($16.8 million) is for LTC ombudsman activities.[42] (See **Table 6**.) The purpose of the LTC Ombudsman Program is to investigate and resolve complaints of residents of nursing facilities, board and care facilities,

---

[41] HHS, AOA, *Fiscal Year 2013 Justification of Estimates for Appropriations Committee*, p. 80.

[42] State allocation tables are at AOA, *Funding Allocations to States and Tribal Organizations*, http://www.aoa.gov/AoARoot/AoA_Programs/OAA/Aging_Network/State_Allocations/index.aspx.

---

and other adult care homes. In FY2010, ombudsmen handled 212,000 complaints, conducted investigations on 143,000 cases, and provided 381,000 consultations to individuals and long-term care facilities.[43]

Table 6. Funding for Older Americans Act, Title VII:
FY2011, FY2012, and FY2013 Budget Request and Continuing Resolution

($ in millions)

	FY2011	FY2012	+/- FY2011	FY2013 Request	FY2013 CR
Title VII: Vulnerable Elder Rights Protection Activities	**$21.839**	**$21.797**	**-$0.042** **-0.2%**	**$21.797**	**$21.797**
Long-term care ombudsman program	16.793	16.761	-0.032 -0.2%	16.761	16.761
Elder abuse prevention	5.046	5.036	-0.010 -0.2%	5.036	5.036
Native Americans elder rights program	—	0ª	—	1.000	0

Source: HHS, AOA, *Fiscal Year 2013 Justification of Estimates for Appropriations Committee*, February 13, 2012, http://aoa.gov/AoARoot/About/Budget/DOCS/FY_2013_AoA_CJ_Feb_2012.pdf; ACL, *Operating Plan for FY2013*, November, 2012.

Notes: FY2012 amounts reflect the 0.189% rescission required by P.L. 112-74, Division F, Section 527.

a. The administration's FY2012 budget request had proposed $1.5 million to support research and demonstration programs addressing elder abuse in tribal nations. The FY2012 Consolidated Appropriations Act did not provide funding for this activity.

For FY2012, Title VII funding levels are relatively similar to FY2011 taking into account the 0.189% across-the-board rescission required for most Labor-HHS-Education line items by the FY2012 Consolidated Appropriations Act. For FY2013, the budget request proposes $22.8 million for Title VII, a $1.0 million (5%) increase over the FY2012 funding level. This increase is due to proposed new funding for research and demonstration programs addressing elder abuse in tribal nations.[44] The CR maintains Title VII funding at the FY2012 level.

Other Aging Services Programs Administered by ACL

The ACL also administers several aging services programs authorized under the Public Health Service Act (PHSA). These programs are the Alzheimer's Disease Supportive Services Program and the Lifespan Respite Care Program. ACL also receives funds for Chronic Disease Self-

---

[43] HHS, AOA, Aging Network, *Aging Integrated Database (AGID)*, National Ombudsman Reporting System, Total Counts, Cases Opened and Total Number of Complaints; Other Ombudsman Activities, Total Number of Consultations to Facilities and Individuals: 50 States + DC & Territories, http://www.data.aoa.gov/. More background on the ombudsman program can be found in CRS Report RS21297, *Older Americans Act: Long-Term Care Ombudsman Program*, by Kirsten J. Colello.

[44] HHS, AOA, *Fiscal Year 2013 Justification of Estimates for Appropriations Committee*, p. 127. S.Rept. 112-176, pp. 142-143. Budget documents include this funding in the total for the Adult Protective Services Demonstration Program.

Management Programs, the National Clearinghouse for Long-Term Care Information, certain activities to carry out the National Plan to Address Alzheimer's Disease, and Elder Abuse Prevention Intervention. (See **Table 7.**) These programs and activities are described in greater detail below.[45]

Table 7. Funding for Other Aging Services Programs Administered by ACL: FY2011, FY2012, and FY2013 Budget Request and Continuing Resolution

($ in millions)

	FY2011	FY2012	+/- FY2011	FY2013 Request	FY2013 CR[a]
Alzheimer's Disease Supportive Services Program (PHSA)	$11.441	$4.011	-$7.430 -64.9%	$9.537	$4.010
Lifespan Respite Care (PHSA)	2.495	2.490	-0.005 -0.2%	2.490	2.490
Chronic Disease Self-Management Programs (ACA, PPHF transfer, mandatory)	0	10.000	+10.000	10.000	na
National Clearinghouse for Long-Term Care Information (DRA, mandatory)	3.000	3.000	0	3.000	na
Medicare Enrollment Assistance Activities	0	0	0	0	na
National Plan to Address Alzheimer's Disease (ACA, PPHF transfer, mandatory)	—	4.000	+4.000	14.700	na
Adult Protective Services Demonstrations (SSA)	—	0[b]	—	7.000	—
State Health Insurance and Assistance Program (OBRA 90)	—	—	—	51.902	—
Elder Abuse Prevention Intervention (ACA, PPHF transfer, mandatory)	—	6.000	+6.000	—	na

Source: HHS, AOA, *Fiscal Year 2013 Justification of Estimates for Appropriations Committee*, February 13, 2012, http://aoa.gov/AoARoot/About/Budget/DOCS/FY_2013_AoA_CJ_Feb_2012.pdf; Personal communication with Michael Bernier, HHS Budget Office, May 16, 2012; ACL, *Operating Plan for FY2013*, November, 2012.

Notes: na = not applicable.

a. The CR provides discretionary funding; it does not provide for mandatory funding or fund transfers.

b. The FY2012 President's budget request proposed $15.0 million in funding for AOA to administer the Adult Protective Services (APS) State Demonstrations. The FY2012 Consolidated Appropriations Act did not provide funding for this activity.

---

[45] ACL also administers programs for persons with disabilities, such as programs under the Developmental Disabilities Assistance and Bill of Rights Act (DD Act). However, this report focuses on programs targeted to the older population and programs historically administered by AOA. In the past, AOA has also received funding to organize and convene the White House Conference on Aging, which, once a decade, makes aging policy recommendations to the President and to Congress. The last conference occurred in 2005 and was authorized under the OAA Amendments of 2000 (P.L. 106-501).

Alzheimer's Disease Supportive Services Program

The Alzheimer's Disease Supportive Services Program (ADSSP)[46] is authorized under Sections 398 and 398B of the PHSA. ADSSP aims to improve and expand evidence-based interventions for persons with Alzheimer's disease and related disorders and their caregivers. The program provides grants to states to expand activities that provide information, education, and assistance to persons affected by Alzheimer's disease through state's systems for home and community-based long-term care services and supports. Although the authorization of appropriations under PHSA Section 398B expired in FY2002, Congress continues to appropriate funding for these activities.[47] ADSSPs received $11.4 million in FY2011, which funded 36 grants to states. For FY2012, ADSSPs received $4.0 million, which is $7.4 million (or 65%) less than FY2011 funding levels. According to AOA, funding for FY2012 was sufficient to continue funding of 11 current grantees.[48] The FY2013 budget request proposes to fund the program at $9.5 million. The CR funds the program at an annualized level of $4.010 million, which is close to the FY2012 level.

Lifespan Respite Care Program

The Lifespan Respite Care Program awards matching grants to eligible state agencies to (1) develop or enhance lifespan respite care activities at the state and local levels; (2) improve the statewide dissemination and coordination of respite care; and (3) provide, supplement, or improve access and quality of respite care services to family caregivers who are caring for children and adults. The law defines "respite care" as planned or emergency care provided to a child or adult of any age with a special need in order to give temporary relief to the family caregiver. The program was enacted under the Lifespan Respite Care Act of 2006 (P.L. 109-442), which amended the PHSA to create a new Title XXIX. PHSA Title XXIX authorizes appropriations totaling $289 million for FY2007 through FY2011.[49] Congress first appropriated funding for Lifespan Respite Care Program activities in FY2009. Between 2009 and 2011, AOA awarded Lifespan Respite Care grants to 30 states.[50] In FY2011, eight states were awarded additional grant funding to focus on the provision of respite services.

In FY2011, the Lifespan Respite Care Program was funded at just under $2.5 million. Although the authorization of appropriations under PHSA Title XXIX expired in FY2011, Congress continues to appropriate funding for these activities. For FY2012, funding levels were relatively similar taking into account the 0.189% across-the-board rescission required for most Labor-HHS-Education line items by the FY2012 Consolidated Appropriations Act. The FY2013 budget request proposes to fund the program at the FY2012 funding level and the CR maintains funding at this level.

---

[46] Formerly known as the Alzheimer's Disease Demonstration Grants to States Program.

[47] 42 U.S.C. 280c-3 to 280c-5.

[48] More information about the Alzheimer's Disease Support Services Program is on the AOA website at http://www.aoa.gov/AoARoot/AoA_Programs/HPW/Alz_Grants/index.aspx.

[49] The PHSA authorizes appropriations of $53.3 million for FY2009, $71.1 million for FY2010, and $94.8 million for FY2011 (42 U.S.C. 300ii-4).

[50] More information about the Lifespan Respite Care Program is on the AOA website at http://www.aoa.gov/AoARoot/AoA_Programs/HCLTC/LRCP/index.aspx.

Chronic Disease Self-Management Programs

Chronic Disease Self-Management Programs (CDSMPs) promote evidence-based disease prevention models that aim to help individuals self-manage their chronic conditions (including diabetes, obesity, cancer, arthritis, and depression) in an effort to reduce the need for more costly health care services and interventions. The initiative builds on AOA's Evidence-Based Disease Prevention Programs, which included CDSMPs, previously funded under AOA budget authority under Aging Network Support Activities and Program Innovations activities. In FY2010, AOA received $32.5 million in American Recovery and Reinvestment Act (ARRA; P.L. 111-5) funds in coordination with the Centers for Disease Control and Prevention (CDC) for CDSMPs for use in FY2010 and FY2011. These funds were transferred to AOA from $650 million that ARRA had provided to HHS for evidence-based prevention and wellness programs.

Of the $32.5 million for CDSMPs, $27.0 million was for cooperative agreements with SUAs and State Departments of Health to deploy such activities. CDSMP activities also received $2.5 million for an interagency agreement with CMS to develop a quality assurance program, and $3.0 million to continue funding a National Technical Assistance Center on Evidence-Based Prevention Programs. CDSMP funding has been awarded through competitive grants to states. In FY2010 AOA funded 47 state CDSMP grants. According to AOA, as of January 2012, just under 62,000 individuals have completed a CDSMP course nationally.[51] This figure is ahead of the program goal of 50,000 individuals completing a CDSMP course within two years of the grant award.

Funding appropriated for FY2011 under the full-year CR (P.L. 112-10) and for FY2012 under the Consolidated Appropriations Act, 2012 (P.L. 112-74) prohibits the use of the act's AOA budget authority for CDSMPs, except to administer already-existing grants that were awarded prior to enactment. FY2012 funds were provided for CDSMPs through transfer of funding from the Prevention and Public Health Fund (PPHF) established under ACA Section 4002. For FY2013, the President's budget proposes $10 million for grants to support CDSMPs through the transfer of funds from the PPHF.[52]

National Clearinghouse for Long-Term Care Information

The National Clearinghouse for Long-Term Care Information (Clearinghouse) was established under the Deficit Reduction Act of 2005 (DRA; P.L. 109-171). Under Section 6021(d) of the DRA, the HHS Secretary is required to establish the Clearinghouse to (1) educate consumers with respect to the availability and limitations of coverage for long-term care under Medicaid; (2) provide objective information to assist consumers in the decision about whether to purchase LTCI; and (3) maintain a list of states with state long-term care partnerships under Medicaid. Congress provided $3 million in mandatory funding for the Clearinghouse for each of FY2006 through FY2010. The ACA amended Section 6021(d) of the DRA to extend this mandatory funding of $3 million per year for FY2011 through FY2015 for the Clearinghouse, among other things.

---

[51] HHS, AOA, Fiscal *Year 2013 Justification of Estimates for Appropriations Committee*, February 13, 2012, p. 178.

[52] For more information about the PPHF see Appendix B in CRS Report R41737, *Public Health Service (PHS) Agencies: Overview and Funding, FY2010-FY2012*, coordinated by C. Stephen Redhead and Pamela W. Smith; and the CRS memorandum *Overview of the Prevention and Public Health Fund (PPHF)*, by Sarah Lister (available by request).

FY2011 funding of $3 million was provided to AOA through a reimbursable agreement from CMS to administer the Clearinghouse. The President's FY2013 budget request indicated that similar funding levels for FY2012 and FY2013 would be provided directly to AOA for Clearinghouse program administration. The American Taxpayer Relief Act of 2012 (ATRA; P.L. 112-240) enacted January 2, 2013, had the effect of canceling the Clearinghouse funding for FY2014 and FY2015 and rescinding any unobligated balances of Clearinghouse funds for FY2013.[53]

Medicare Enrollment Assistance Activities

ATRA, P.L. 112-240, extends funding under Section 119 of the Medicare Improvements for Patients and Providers Act of 2008 (MIPPA; P.L. 110-275) to provide $25.0 million in mandatory FY2013 funding for outreach and education activities to beneficiaries eligible for or receiving services under Medicare low-income assistance programs. These Medicare enrollment assistance activities are conducted through State Health Insurance and Assistance Programs (SHIPs), AAAs, ADRCs, and the National Center for Benefits Outreach and Enrollment. The HHS Secretary is authorized to enlist these entities' support to conduct outreach aimed at preventing disease and promoting wellness as an additional use of these funds.

Of the $25.0 million in FY2013 funding, $7.5 million is allocated to SHIPs, $7.5 million is allocated to AAAs, $5.0 million is allocated to ADRCs, and $5.0 million is allocated to the National Center for Benefits Outreach and Enrollment.[54]

National Plan to Address Alzheimer's Disease

In May 2012, HHS released the National Plan to Address Alzheimer's Disease, a report mandated by the National Alzheimer's Project Act (P.L. 111-375).[55] To assist in carrying out the plan's goals, the Obama Administration separately announced a new $156 million investment of federal funds to address Alzheimer's disease.[56] The investment includes $18.7 million to AOA, funded through the PPHF. According to HHS, the following activities will receive funding:

- $8.2 million for education and outreach to enhance public awareness of Alzheimer's disease ($4 million in FY2012 and $4.2 million in FY2013); and

---

[53] P.L. 112-240 section 642(b)(3) amended Section 6021(d) of the DRA to read as it had prior to enactment of the ACA.

[54] Funding for these activities was first provided by Section 119 of the Medicare Improvements for Patients and Providers Act of 2008 (MIPPA; P.L. 110-275), which provided $25 million for FY2009. ACA section 3306 extended MIPPA Section 119 to provide an additional $45.0 million for the period of FY2010 through FY2012. Of the $45.0 million, $15.0 million was allocated to SHIPs, $15.0 million was allocated to AAAs, $10.0 million was allocated to ADRCs, and $5.0 million was allocated to the National Center for Benefits and Outreach Enrollment. (ACA allocated the funds to these entities in the same proportion as under MIPPA). In FY2010, $15.0 million was sent to CMS for SHIPs, and $30.0 million was transferred to AOA for the other entities. No additional funds were provided for these activities in FY2011 or FY2012.

[55] HHS, *National Plan to Address Alzheimer's Disease*, May 15, 2012, http://aspe.hhs.gov/daltcp/napa/NatlPlan.pdf.

[56] HHS, "We can't wait: Administration announces new steps to fight Alzheimer's disease," press release, February 7, 2012, http://www.hhs.gov/news/press/2012pres/02/20120207a.html; HHS, *National Plan to Address Alzheimer's Disease*, p. 3.

- $10.5 million in FY2013 to expand supports for people with Alzheimer's disease and their caregivers in the community.[57]

The above funds would be specifically for implementing the National Plan to Address Alzheimer's Disease. According to HHS, the activities would be distinct in goals and participants from AOA's existing ADSSP activities.[58]

Elder Abuse Prevention Intervention

In FY2012, the HHS Secretary transferred $6.0 million from the PPHF for new grants to states and tribes to test elder abuse prevention strategies.[59] ACL awarded grants to eight state and tribal organizations. Projects included using forensic accountants to prevent elder financial exploitation, increasing medication adherence to prevent elder self-neglect, and developing screening tools to identify elder abuse.[60]

Other Programs Included in the FY2013 Budget Request

The FY2013 budget request proposes that AOA administer two additional programs. If funded, AOA would be responsible for the administration of the Adult Protective Services (APS) State Demonstrations established under the ACA. AOA would also have expanded administrative responsibilities with the proposed transfer of the State Health Insurance and Assistance Program (SHIPs) from CMS to AOA. These programs are described in greater detail below.

Adult Protective Services State Demonstrations

Adult Protective Services State Demonstrations are authorized under Title XX, Section 2042, of SSA as amended by the ACA Section 6703, Elder Justice. Grant awards for APS demonstration programs may be used by state and local governments to test training modules developed for the purpose of detecting or preventing elder abuse; to test methods to detect or prevent financial exploitation and elder abuse; to test whether training on elder abuse forensics enhances the detection of abuse by employees of state or local government; and for other related matters. For each of FY2011 through FY2014, the SSA authorizes to be appropriated $25.0 million for APS State Demonstration grants.

---

[57] Personal communication with Michael Bernier, HHS Budget Office, May 16, 2012; HHS, *National Plan to Address Alzheimer's Disease*, pp. 23, 29; HHS, Prevention and Public Health Fund, FY 2012 Allocation of Funds, http://www.hhs.gov/open/recordsandreports/prevention/index.html

[58] Personal communication with Michael Bernier, HHS Budget Office, May 16, 2012.

[59] States could apply for cooperative agreements under SSA Title XX, Section 2042, as amended under ACA Section 6703. Tribes could apply for cooperative agreements under OAA Section 411. HHS, "HHS grants to help protect seniors, test elder abuse prevention strategies," press release, June 14, 2012, http://www.hhs.gov/news/press/2012pres/06/20120614a.html; AOA, *PPHF – 2012 – Elder Abuse Prevention Interventions Program: Program Announcement and Grant Application Instructions*, OMB Approval No. 0985-0018, 2012, http://aoa.gov/Grants/Funding/docs/2012/FY2012_PA_EA_Prevention_Final_508.pdf; HHS, *Prevention and Public Health Fund, FY 2012 Allocation of Funds*, http://www.hhs.gov/open/recordsandreports/prevention/index.html.

[60] AOA, "Protecting America's Seniors: The Elder Abuse Prevention Interventions Program," press release, November 1, 2012, http://aoa.gov/aoaroot/Press_Room/News/2012/ElderAbusePreventionGrants.pdf.

The FY2013 budget request proposes $7.0 million for APS State Demonstration grants to be administered by AOA; if appropriated, this would be the first year of funding for this program.[61] Of the $7.0 million requested, $5.5 million would fund competitive grants to assist state and local APS programs, and $1.5 million would fund evaluation and data collection activities associated with the APS State demonstration grants.[62]

State Health Insurance and Assistance Programs

The State Health Insurance and Assistance Programs provide state-level funding for counseling and information assistance to Medicare beneficiaries and their families on Medicare and other health insurance issues.[63] The SHIP program is authorized under Section 4360 of the Omnibus Budget Reconciliation Act of 1990.[64] Although the program's authorization of appropriations expired in FY1996, Congress continues to appropriate funding for these activities. Funding is provided through a transfer of discretionary funding from the Federal Hospital Insurance Trust Fund and the Federal Supplementary Medical Insurance Trust Fund. SHIP grants provide funding for states to plan and operate various information, counseling, and assistance activities. Medicare beneficiaries receive assistance through one-on-one counseling both in person and by telephone from paid and volunteer SHIP counselors. SHIP staff also conducts public outreach and education activities to inform beneficiaries about coverage and enrollment options. There are SHIPs in all 50 states, as well as the District of Columbia, Guam, Puerto Rico, and the Virgin Islands. Of the 54 SHIP grant programs, about two-thirds are administered by State Units on Aging established under OAA.[65] According to AOA, in FY2009, the most recent year for which data are available, SHIPs targeted more than 4.7 million individuals through about 55,000 public information and outreach events.

The FY2013 budget request also proposes to transfer administration of SHIPs from CMS to AOA. SHIP funding was $52.0 million in FY2011 and $52.1 million in FY2012. The FY2013 budget request proposes $51.9 million.[66] S. 3295 would implement the program's transfer from CMS and would fund SHIPs at $52.1 million in FY2013, the same as the FY2012 level.

---

[61] The FY2012 President's budget request proposed $15.0 million in funding for AOA to administer the Adult Protective Services (APS) State Demonstrations. The FY2012 Consolidated Appropriations Act did not provide funding for this activity.

[62] The FY2013 budget request and S. 3295 propose an additional $1.0 million in new Title VII funds to support research and demonstration programs to assist Tribal nations with addressing elder abuse and related issues.

[63] More information about SHIPs is on the CMS website at https://www.cms.gov/partnerships/10_SHIPS.asp.

[64] 42 U.S.C. 1395b-4.

[65] The National Health Policy Forum, *The Basics: The State Health Insurance Assistance Program (SHIP)*, prepared by Carol V. O'Shaughnessy, Washington, DC, March 29, 2010, http://www.nhpf.org/library/the-basics/Basics_SHIP_03-29-10.pdf.

[66] The FY2012 budget request similarly proposed transferring the administration of SHIPs from CMS to AOA. The conference report accompanying the FY2012 Consolidated Appropriations Act states that "The conferees have not transferred the SHIP program from CMS." H.Rept. 112-331, *Military Construction and Veterans Affairs and Related Agencies Appropriations Act, 2012, Conference Report to accompany H.R. 2055*, p. 1145.

Appendix A. Older Americans Act and Other Aging Services Programs: Funding for FY2011 and FY2012, and FY2013 Budget Request

Table A-1 provides details of funding for programs authorized by OAA and other aging services programs that are administered by ACL but that receive funds under non-OAA authorities. The table includes funding levels for FY2011 and FY2012, as well as changes from FY2011 to FY2012. It also includes proposed FY2013 funding levels under the following: (1) the President's FY2013 Budget; and (2) annualized FY2013 funding levels under the Continuing Appropriations Resolution, 2013 (CR; P.L. 112-175), as detailed in ACL and DOL Operating Plans released in November 2012. The table also includes funding for specific activities within a larger budget line—in italicized font with appropriations amounts in parentheses.

The FY2013 CR funding levels are not final. The CR provides funding from October 1, 2012 through March 27, 2013. There is uncertainty depending on whether certain actions, such as sequestration, are taken pursuant to the Budget Control Act (BCA; P.L. 112-25) and the American Taxpayer Relief Act of 2012 (ATRA; P.L. 112-240). Also, the agencies have some authority to request additional funds and to transfer funds among programs.

Table A-1. Funding for Older Americans Act (OAA) and Other Administration for Community Living (ACL) Aging Services Programs: FY2011, FY2012, and FY2013 Budget Request and Continuing Resolution

($ in millions)

	FY2011	FY2012	+/- FY2011	FY2013 Request	FY2013 CR[a]
Title II: Administration on Aging	**$40.075**	**$43.160**	**+$3.085 +7.7%**	**$36.899**	**$43.160**
Program Administration	19.939	23.063	+3.124 +15.7%	23.259	23.063
Senior Medicare Patrol [b]	9.420	9.402	-0.018 -0.2%	9.402	9.402
Aging Network Support Activities (Title II portion)[c]	2.891	2.886	-0.006 -0.2%	2.886	2.886
Elder Rights Support Activities (Title II portion)[d]	1.355	1.352	-0.003 -0.2%	1.352	1.352
Aging and Disability Resource Centers[e]	6.469	6.457	-0.012 -0.2%	0	6.457
Title III: Grants for State and Community Programs on Aging	**$1,360.342**	**$1,357.772**	**-$2.570 -0.2%**	**$1,357.772**	**$1,357.770**
Nutrition services	817.835	816.290	-1.545 -0.2%	816.290	816.289
Supportive services and centers	367.611	366.916	-0.695 -0.2%	366.916	366.916
Family caregivers	153.912	153.621	-0.291 -0.2%	153.621	153.621
Disease prevention/health promotion	20.984	20.945	-0.039 -0.2%	20.945	20.944
Title IV: Activities for Health, Independence, and Longevity	**$27.102**	**$7.723**	**-$19.378 -71.5%**	**$7.723**	**$7.723**
Aging Network Support Activities (Title IV portion)	5.292	4.988	-0.305 -5.8%	4.988	4.988
Elder Rights Support Activities (Title IV portion)	2.741	2.736	-0.005 -0.2%	2.736	2.736
Program Innovations[f]	19.069	0	-19.069 -100%	0	0
Title V: Community Service Employment for Older Americans	**$449.100**	**$448.251**	**-$0.849 -0.2%**	**$448.251**	**$448.251**
Title VI: Grants to Native Americans	**$34.029**	**$33.965**	**-$0.064 -0.2%**	**$33.965**	**$33.965**
Supportive and nutrition services	27.653	27.601	-0.052 -0.2%	27.601	27.601
Native American family caregivers	6.376	6.364	-0.012 -0.2%	6.364	6.364

	FY2011	FY2012	+/- FY2011	FY2013 Request	FY2013 CR[a]
Title VII: Vulnerable Elder Rights Protection Activities	$21.839	$21.797	-$0.042 -0.2%	$22.797	$21.797
Long-term care ombudsman program	16.793	16.761	-0.032 -0.2%	16.761	16.761
Elder abuse prevention	5.046	5.036	-0.010 -0.2%	5.036	5.036
Native Americans elder rights program	—	0[g]	—	1.000	0
TOTAL: Older Americans Act Programs	**$1,932.487**	**$1,912.668**	**-$19.819 -1.0%**	**$1,907.407**	**$1,912.666**
Funding to ACL From Non-OAA Authorities					
Alzheimer's Disease Supportive Services Program (PHSA)	$11.441	$4.011	-7.430 -64.9%	$9.537	$4.010
Lifespan Respite Care (PHSA)	2.495	2.490	-0.005 -0.2%	2.490	2.490
Senior Medicare Patrol Program (HCFAC, mandatory)[h]	3.312	10.710	+7.398 +223.4%	10.710	na
Aging and Disability Resource Centers (ACA, mandatory)[i]	10.000	10.000	0	10.000	na
Chronic Disease Self-Management Programs (ACA, PPHF transfer, mandatory)[j]	0	10.000	+10.000	10.000	na
National Clearinghouse for Long-Term Care Information (DRA, mandatory)	3.000	3.000	0	3.000	na
Medicare Enrollment Assistance Activities (MIPPA, ACA, ATRA, mandatory)[k]	0	0	—	0	na
National Plan to Address Alzheimer's Disease (ACA, PPHF transfer, mandatory)[l]	—	4.000	+4.000	14.700	na
Adult Protective Services Demonstrations (SSA)	—	0	—	7.000	—
State Health Insurance and Assistance Program (OBRA 90)[m]	—	—	—	51.902	—
Elder Abuse Prevention Intervention (ACA, PPHF transfer, mandatory)[n]	—	6.000	—	—	na
Total ACL Administered Aging Services Programs (discretionary)	**$1,497.322**	**$1,470.918**	**-$26.404 -1.8%**	**$1,978.336**	**$1,470.915**
Total ACL Administered Aging Services Programs (mandatory and discretionary)	**$1,513.634**	**$1,514.628**	**+$0.994 +0.07%**	**$2,026.746**	**$1,470.915**

Source: HHS, AOA, *Fiscal Year 2013 Justification of Estimates for Appropriations Committee*, February 13, 2012, pp. 22-23, 36-37, 152, http://aoa.gov/AoARoot/About/Budget/DOCS/FY_2013_AoA_CJ_Feb_2012.pdf; S.Rept. 112-176, pp. 23, 139-145, 241, 262-263; Personal communication with G. Steven Hagy, Director, Office of Budget and Finance, AOA, April 4, 2012; Personal communication with Michael Bernier, HHS Budget Office, May 16, 2012; ACL and DOL, *Operating Plans for FY2013*, November 2012.

Notes: na = not applicable. The ACL Operating Plan for FY2013 does not break down funding by OAA Title. CRS assumes that each program's funding levels would remain the same as in FY2012.

a. The Continuing Appropriations Resolution, 2013 (CR, P.L. 112-175) provides discretionary funding from October 1, 2012 through March 27, 2013. For most programs receiving discretionary appropriations, the CR maintains annualized funding at the FY2012 levels provided by the FY2012 Consolidated Appropriations Act (P.L. 112-74), plus an increase of 0.612%. OMB announced that during the CR period, the FY2012 base level of funding would be automatically apportioned, except for the 0.612%. Instead, agencies would have to submit a written request to OMB to obtain these funds. (OMB, Apportionment of the Continuing Resolution(s) for Fiscal Year 2013, OMB Bulletin No. 12-02, September 28, 2012, http://www.whitehouse.gov/sites/default/files/omb/bulletins/fy2012/b12-02.pdf). Consequently, the FY2013 ACL and DOL Operating Plans do not reflect the 0.612% increase. Likewise, this table reflects the base level of funding; the numbers exclude the 0.612% increase. The amounts in this table are annualized.

b. The Senior Medicare Patrol program is listed under Title II, so as to be consistent with the AOA FY2013 Justification (pp. 36 and 145). Per personal communication with AOA, the Senior Medicare Patrol program receives funds under Title IV authority.

c. Title II Aging Network Support Activities include the National Eldercare Locator and the Pension Information and Counseling Program. Title IV Aging Network Support Activities include the National Alzheimer's Call Center, the National Education & Resource Center on Women & Retirement, National Resource Centers on Native Americans, National Minority Aging Organizations, National Technical Assistance Resource Center for Lesbian, Gay, Bisexual, and Transgender (LGBT) Elders, Multigenerational Civic Engagement, and Program Performance and Technical Assistance.

d. Title II Elder Rights Support Activities include the National Long-Term Care Ombudsman Resource Center and the National Center on Elder Abuse. Title IV Elder Rights Support Activities include Model Approaches to Statewide Legal Systems and National Legal Assistance and Support Projects.

e. Aging and Disability Resource Center (ADRC) discretionary funding is listed under Title II, reflecting the OAA statute (§202(b)(8)) and for consistency with the AOA FY2013 Justification (p. 158). Per personal communication with AOA, ADRCs receive discretionary funds under Title IV authority.

f. Program Innovations funding included Health and Long-Term Care Programs (excluding ADRCs) and Community Innovations for Aging in Place.

g. The administration's FY2012 budget request had proposed $1.5 million to support research and demonstration programs addressing elder abuse in tribal nations. The FY2012 Consolidated Appropriations Act did not provide funding for this activity.

h. Health Care Fraud and Abuse Control (HCFAC) funds have historically been provided to the Senior Medicare Patrol Program. HCFAC funds are distributed to anti-fraud activities from the Medicare Trust Fund at the joint discretion of the HHS Secretary and Attorney General. The AOA FY2013 budget proposal lists as "a placeholder" $10.710 million; the final FY2013 amount will be determined by the HHS Secretary and Attorney General. In addition, the Senior Medicare Patrol program receives funding under Title II of the OAA.

i. Sec. 2405 of the Patient Protection and Affordable Care Act (ACA, P.L. 111-148, as amended), provided mandatory appropriations for ADRCs of $10.0 million for each year from FY2010 to FY2014. In addition, ADRCs receive funding under OAA Title II: $6.469 million in FY2011 and $6.457 million in FY2012. No discretionary funding for ADRC's is requested for FY2013.

j. For Chronic Disease Self-Management Programs (CDSMPs), FY2012 funds were provided and FY2013 funds are requested under the authority of PHSA Sec. 311 (42 U.S.C. §243, on general authority for cooperation), PHSA Sec. 317(k)(2) (42 U.S.C. §247b(k)(2) on preventive health services project grants), and ACA Sec. 4002 (42 U.S.C. §300u-11, on the Prevention and Public Health Fund, PPHF). For more information about the PPHF see Appendix B in CRS Report R41737, *Public Health Service (PHS) Agencies: Overview and Funding, FY2010-FY2012*, coordinated by C. Stephen Redhead and Pamela W. Smith; and the CRS memorandum Overview of the Prevention and Public Health Fund (PPHF), by Sarah Lister (available by request). In FY2010, AOA received $32.5 million in American Recovery and Reinvestment Act (ARRA, P.L. 111-5) funds for CDSMPs for use in FY2010 and FY2011. These funds were transferred to AOA from $650 million that ARRA had provided to HHS for evidence-based prevention and wellness programs.

k. The American Taxpayer Relief Act of 2012 (ATRA) extends Section 119 of the Medicare Improvements for Patients and Providers Act of 2008 (MIPPA) to provide $25.0 million in FY2013 funding for outreach and education to those eligible for Medicare low-income assistance programs. Of that amount, $7.5 million is allocated to SHIPs, and the rest is allocated to ACL-administered activities: $7.5 million to AAAs, $5.0 million to ADRCs, and $5.0 million to the National Center for Benefits Outreach and Enrollment.

l. Per personal communication with the HHS Budget Office, HHS plans to transfer funds to AOA from the PPHF to carry out certain goals of the National Plan to Address Alzheimer's Disease. Under this plan, AOA would receive $4 million in FY2012 and $4.2 million in FY2013 for education and outreach to enhance public awareness of Alzheimer's disease. AOA would also receive $10.5 million in FY2013 to expand supports for people with Alzheimer's disease and their caregivers in the community.

m. The FY2013 budget request proposes to transfer administration of the State Health Insurance and Assistance Program (SHIP) from CMS to AOA. The SHIP program is authorized under Sec. 4360 of the Omnibus Budget Reconciliation Act of 1990 (OBRA 90, 42 U.S.C. §1395b-4). While authorizations of appropriations under the act expired in FY1996, the program continues to receive funding. SHIP funding was $52.0 million in FY2011 and $52.1 million in FY2012.

n. In FY2012, $6 million was transferred to ACL from PPHF to pilot test interventions to prevent elder abuse, neglect, and exploitation." HHS, Prevention and Public Health Fund, FY 2012 Allocation of Funds, http://www.hhs.gov/open/recordsandreports/prevention/index.html; HHS, "HHS grants to help protect seniors, test elder abuse prevention strategies," press release, June 14, 2012, http://www.hhs.gov/news/press/2012pres/06/20120614a.html; AOA, PPHF – 2012 – Elder Abuse Prevention Interventions Program: Program Announcement and Grant Application Instructions, OMB Approval No. 0985-0018, 2012, http://aoa.gov/Grants/Funding/docs/2012/FY2012_PA_EA_Prevention_Final_508.pdf; AOA, "Protecting America's Seniors: The Elder Abuse Prevention Interventions Program," press release, November 1, 2012, http://aoa.gov/aoaroot/Press_Room/News/2012/ElderAbusePreventionGrants.pdf

Appendix B. Older Americans Act and Other AOA Programs: FY2004-FY2012 Funding

Table B-1 shows the appropriations history for the act's programs for FY2004 through FY2012. The appropriations histories for selected other programs administered by AOA are also provided. The table also includes funding for specific activities within a larger budget line – in italicized font with appropriations amounts in parentheses.

Table B-1. Funding for the Older Americans Act (OAA) and Other Administration on Aging (AOA) Programs: FY2004-FY2012

($ in millions)

OAA Programs and Selected Other AOA Programs	FY2004	FY2005[a]	FY2006[b]	FY2007[c]	FY2008[d]	FY2009[e]	FY2010[f]	FY2011[g]	FY2012[h]
Title II: Administration on Aging	**$30.618**	**$31.567**	**$30.812**	**$31.518**	**$49.653**	**$60.390**	**$64.252**	**$40.075**	**$43.160**
Program administration	17.324	18.301	17.688	18.385	18.064	18.696	19.976	19.939	23.063
Aging network support activities	13.294	13.266	13.124	13.133	31.589[i]	41.694[j]	44.276	2.891[k]	2.886[k]
Senior Medicare Patrol	—	—	—	—	—	—	—	9.420[l]	9.402[l]
Aging and Disability Resource Centers	—	—	—	—	—	—	—	6.469[l]	6.457[l]
Elder rights support activities[m]	—	—	—	—	—	—	—	1.355	1.352
Title III: Grants for State and Community Programs on Aging	**$1,243.059**	**1,250.192**	**$1,242.378**	**$1,263.232**	**$1,283.816**	**$1,443.337**[n]	**$1,362.866**	**$1,360.342**	**$1,357.772**
Supportive services and centers	353.889	354.136	350.354	350.595	351.348	361.348	368.290	367.611	366.916
Family caregivers[o]	152.738	155.744	156.060	156.167	153.439	154.220	154.197	153.912	153.621
Disease prevention/health promotion	21.970	21.616	21.385	21.400	21.026	21.026	21.026	20.984	20.945
Nutrition services	714.462	718.696	714.579	735.070	758.003	906.743[p]	819.353	817.835	816.290
Congregate meals (non-add)	(386.353)	(387.274)	(385.054)	(398.919)[q]	(410.716)	(499.269)[r]	(440.718)	(439.901)	(439.070)
Home-delivered meals (non-add)	(179.917)	(182.826)	(181.781)	(188.305)[q]	(193.858)	(246.459)[s]	(217.644)	(217.241)	(216.831)
Nutrition services incentive grants (non-add)	(148.192)	(148.596)	(147.744)	(147.846)	(153.429)	(161.015)	(160.991)	(160.693)	(160.389)
Title IV: Activities for Health, Independence, and Longevity[c]	**$33.509**	**$43.286**	**$24.578**	**$24.058**	**$14.655**	**$18.172**	**$19.020**	**$27.102**	**$7.723**
Program Innovations	33.509	43.286	24.578	24.058	14.655	18.172	19.020	19.069	0
Elder rights support activities[m]	—	—	—	—	—	—	—	2.741	2.736

OAA Programs and Selected Other AOA Programs	FY2004	FY2005[a]	FY2006[b]	FY2007[c]	FY2008[d]	FY2009[e]	FY2010[f]	FY2011[g]	FY2012[h]
Aging network support activities[u]	—	—	—	—	—	—	—	5.292	4.988
Title V: Community Service Employment for Older Americans	$438.650	$436.678	$432.311	$483.611[q]	$521.625	$691.925[v]	$825.425[w]	$449.100	$448.251
Title VI: Grants to Native Americans	$32.771	$32.702	$32.353	$32.375	$33.214	$36.597[x]	$34.092	$34.029	$33.965
Supportive and nutrition services	26.453	26.398	26.116	26.134	26.898	30.208[y]	27.704	27.653	27.601
Native American caregivers	6.318	6.304	6.237	6.241	6.316	6.389	6.388	6.376	6.364
Title VII: Vulnerable Elder Rights Protection Activities	$19.444	$19.288	$20.142	$20.156	$20.633	$21.383	$21.880	$21.839	$21.797
Long-term care ombudsman program	14.276	14.162	15.000	15.010	15.577[z]	16.327	16.825	16.793	16.761
Elder abuse prevention	5.168	5.126	5.142	5.146	5.056	5.056	5.055	5.046	5.036
Legal assistance	0	0	0	0	0	0	0	0	0
Native Americans elder rights program	0	0	0	0	0	0	0	0	0
TOTAL Older Americans Act Programs	$1,798.051	$1,813.713	$1,782.574	$1,854.950	$1,923.596	$2,271.804[aa]	$2,327.535	$1,932.487	$1,912.668
Alzheimer's Disease Supportive Services Program[bb]	11.883	11.786	11.660	11.668	11.464	11.464	11.462	11.441	4.011
White House Conference on Aging	2.814[cc]	4.520[cc]	0[cc]	0	0	0	0	0	0
Lifespan Respite Care[dd]	—	—	—	0	0	2.500	2.500	2.495	2.490
Senior Medicare Patrol Program (HCFAC, mandatory)	3.276	3.128	3.128	3.128	3.128	3.200	3.779	3.312[ee]	10.710[ee]
Aging and Disability Resource Centers (ACA, mandatory)[ff]	—	—	—	—	—	—	10.000	10.000	10.000

OAA Programs and Selected Other AOA Programs	FY2004	FY2005[a]	FY2006[b]	FY2007[c]	FY2008[d]	FY2009[e]	FY2010[f]	FY2011[g]	FY2012[h]
Chronic Disease Self-Management Programs (ARRA, ACA, PPHF transfer, mandatory)[gg]	—	—	—	—	—	—	32.500	—	10.000
National Clearinghouse for Long-Term Care Information (DRA, mandatory)[hh]	—	—	—	—	—	—	—	3.000	3.000
Medicare Enrollment Assistance Activities (MIPPA, ACA, ATRA, mandatory)	—	—	—	—	—	$17.500[kk]	$30.000[ll]	—	—
National Plan to Address Alzheimer's Disease (ACA, PPHF transfer, mandatory)[ii]	—	—	—	—	—	—	—	—	4.000
Elder Abuse Prevention Intervention (SSA, ACA, PPHF transfer, mandatory)[jj]	—	—	—	—	—	—	—	—	6.000

Source: FY2004-FY2006: Appropriations legislation and committee reports, various years. FY2007-FY2008: Consolidated Appropriations Act, 2008, Committee Print of the Committee on Appropriations, U.S. House of Representatives, on H.R. 2764/P.L. 110-161, January, 2008, pp. 1776, 1809-1810, http://www.gpo.gov/fdsys/granule/CPRT-110HPRT39564/CPRT-110HPRT39564-DivisionA/content-detail.html. FY2009: "Explanatory Statement Submitted by Mr. Obey, Chairman of the House Committee on Appropriations, Regarding H.R. 1105, Omnibus Appropriations Act, 2009," *Congressional Record*, February 23, 2009, pp. H2372, H2385; H.Rept. 111-16, *Conference Report to Accompany H.R. 1*, pp. 449, 455. FY2010-FY2012: HHS, *Department of Health and Human Services – FY2011 Operating Plans*; DOL, *Department of Labor, FY2011 Operating Plan*, http://www.dol.gov/dol/budget/2012/PDF/2011OperatingPlanTable.pdf, Personal communication with G. Steven Hagy, director, Office of Budget and Finance, Administration on Aging, March 18 and May 16, 2011, and April 4, 2012; HHS, AOA, Fiscal Year 2013 Justification of Estimates for Appropriations Committee, February 13, 2012, http://aoa.gov/AoARoot/About/Budget/DOCS/FY_2013_AoA_CJ_Feb_2012.pdf; Personal communication with Michael Bernier, HHS Budget Office, May 16, 2012. Senior Medicare Patrol Program (HCFAC): U.S. Department of Justice and U.S. Department of Health and Human Services and U.S. Department of Justice, *Health Care Fraud and Abuse Control Program, Annual Report*, http://oig.hhs.gov/reports-and-publications/hcfac/index.asp.

Notes:

a. FY2005 amounts reflect the 0.80% across-the-board reduction required by P.L. 108-447, Division J, Sec. 122. The Administration was given discretion on how to distribute the reduction among individual accounts and line items.

b. FY2006 amounts reflect two rescissions. (1) A 1% across-the-board reduction required by P.L. 109-148, Division B, Title III, Chapter 8, Sec. 3801. (2) On June 14, 2006, the HHS Secretary notified the Appropriations Committees that he would transfer funds among HHS programs to finance activities related to the Medicare drug benefit call center. This transfer was a 0.069% across-the-board reduction and it reduced Administration on Aging funds by $0.9 million. It was authorized by Sec. 208 of P.L. 109-149.

c. For FY2007, P.L. 110-5 specified dollar amounts for some, but not all, programs. Agencies had some flexibility to determine program amounts based on FY2006 appropriations.

d. P.L. 110-161, the FY2008 Consolidated Appropriations Act, applied an across-the-board reduction of 1.747% to figures in the bill text and Explanatory Statement narrative (Division G, Title V, §528). The table reflects this reduction.

e. FY2009 figures include funds from both the FY2009 Omnibus Appropriations Act (P.L. 111-8) and the American Recovery and Reinvestment Act (ARRA, P.L. 111-5).

f. FY2010 amounts reflect both appropriations and transferred funds, including the HHS Secretary's transfer of $224,298 from AOA to assist states with AIDS Drug Assistance Programs (ADAP). The Secretary reallocated and transferred a total of $25 million from various HHS agencies to assist state ADAP programs with waitlists and cost containment. For more background on the transfer, see HHS, "Statement from Secretary Sebelius on Reallocating $25 million for AIDS Drug Assistance," press release, July 9, 2010, http://www.hhs.gov/news/press/2010pres/07/201000709c.html, and HHS, Health Resources and Services Administration, *Fiscal Year 2012 Justification of Estimates for Appropriations Committees*, p. 261, http://www.hrsa.gov/about/budget/budgetjustification2012.pdf.

g. FY2011 full-year continuing resolution (CR) P.L. 112-10 specified funding levels for some, but not all, OAA and other AOA-administered programs. For programs not specifically mentioned in the CR, AOA had some discretion in how to allocate FY2011 funds. The CR required agencies, within 30 days of enactment, to submit expenditure and operating plans to congressional appropriations committees, at a level of detail below the account level. FY2011 amounts reflect the 0.2% across-the-board rescission required by Sec. 1119. See HHS, *Department of Health and Human Services – FY2011 Operating Plans*.

h. P.L. 112-74, the FY2012 Consolidated Appropriations Act, Division F, Section 527, applied a 0.189% across-the-board rescission on most Labor-HHS-Education items, including OAA and AOA items. The table reflects this rescission.

i. The Choices for Independence Initiative included newly authorized provisions of the Older Americans Act Amendments of 2006 (P.L. 109-365) related to "aging and disability resource centers (ADRCs), evidence-based prevention programs, and consumer-directed services targeted at individuals who are at high risk of nursing home placement and spend-down to Medicaid" (H.Rept. 110-231, p. 207). The Bush Administration's FY2008 budget requested Choices for Independence funds under Title IV, while the FY2008 Consolidated Appropriations Act (P.L. 110-161) provided the funds under Aging Network support activities under Title II. The President's FY2008 budget request would have provided $28.0 million for Choices for Independence. P.L. 110-161 provided $16.2 million for Choices for Independence (after a 1.747% across-the-board reduction). Choices for Independence was subsequently renamed "Health and Long-Term Care Programs" in the Obama Administration's FY2010 budget request.

j. Includes $28.0 million for Choices for Independence. The Bush Administration's FY2009 budget request would have funded Choices for Independence at $28.0 million under Title IV, which authorizes funds for training, research, and demonstration projects. Choices for Independence was subsequently renamed "Health and Long-Term Care Programs" in the Obama Administration's FY2010 budget request.

k. Several activities that were previously included under Aging Network Support Activities are listed under separate line items starting in FY2011. These activities include the Senior Medicare Patrol Program, ADRCs, the National Center on Elder Abuse (now under Elder rights support activities), and the National Long-Term Care Ombudsman Resource Center (now under Elder rights support activities). For FY2011 and FY2012, Title II Aging Network Support Activities include only the National Eldercare Locator and the Pension Information and Counseling Program.

l. Prior to FY2011, Title II funds to Senior Medicare Patrol and ADRCs are included in the total for Aging Network Support Activities.

m. Elder rights support activities include the National Center on Elder Abuse (authorized under Title II), the National Long-Term Care Ombudsman Resource Center (authorized under Title II), Model Approaches to Statewide Legal Assistance (authorized under Title IV), and National Legal Assistance and Support Projects (authorized under Title IV). Prior to FY2011, funding for these programs was included in totals for Aging Network Support Activities and Program Innovations.

n. Total FY2009 funding for Title III was $1,443.337 million. This includes $1,346.337 million from the FY2009 Omnibus Appropriations Act (P.L. 111-8) and $97.000 million from ARRA.

o. Funding for Native American family caregiving is shown in Title VI.

p. Total FY2009 funding for Title III-C Nutrition Services was $906.743 million. This includes $809.743 million from the FY2009 Omnibus Appropriations Act (P.L. 111-8) and $97.000 million from ARRA.

q. Funding level was specified in P.L. 110-5, Revised Continuing Appropriations Resolution, 2007.

r. Total FY2009 funding for congregate meals was $499.269 million. This includes $434.269 million from the FY2009 Omnibus Appropriations Act (P.L. 111-8) and $65.000 million from ARRA.

s. Total FY2009 funding for home-delivered meals was $246.459 million. This includes $214.459 million from the FY2009 Omnibus Appropriations Act (P.L. 111-8) and $32.000 million from ARRA.

t. The Older Americans Act Amendments of 2006 (P.L. 109-365) renamed Title IV, formerly titled "Training, Research, and Discretionary Projects and Programs." Many activities under Title IV are, at times, also referred to as "Program Innovations."

u. Title IV Aging Network Support Activities include the National Alzheimer's Call Center, the National Education & Resource Center on Women & Retirement, National Resource Centers on Native Americans, National Minority Aging Organizations, and National Technical Assistance Resource Center for Lesbian, Gay, Bisexual, and Transgender (LGBT) Elders, Multigenerational Civic Engagement, and Program Performance and Technical Assistance. In AOA budget documents prior to FY2012, funding for these programs was provided under Program Innovations. In this report, for comparability, the FY2011 and FY2012 columns reflect the categorizations in FY2012 appropriations and FY2013 budget documents.

v. Total FY2009 funding for Title V was $691.925 million. This includes $571.925 million from the FY2009 Omnibus Appropriations Act (P.L. 111-8) and $120.000 million from ARRA.

w. The FY2010 Title V funding level included $225 million that, according to the Department of Labor (DOL), "was intended as a one-time provision related to current economic conditions. The additional funding was provided as a short-term program expansion to support temporary job opportunities for low-income elderly individuals while the nation recovers from the economic downturn." DOL, *FY2011 Congressional Budget Justification, Employment and Training Administration, Community Service Employment for Older Americans* (CSEOA), p. CSEOA-2.

x. Total FY2009 funding for Title VI was $36.597 million. This includes $33.597 million from the FY2009 Omnibus Appropriations Act (P.L. 111-8) and $3.000 million from ARRA.

y. Total FY2009 funding for supportive and nutrition services to Native Americans was $30.208 million. This includes $27.208 million from the FY2009 Omnibus Appropriations Act (P.L. 111-8) and $3.000 million from ARRA.

z. Separate amounts not specified in FY2008 Consolidated Appropriations Act tables. These figures were calculated by CRS by applying the 1.747% across-the-board reduction to figures in the Explanatory Statement narrative in the Congressional Record, December 17, 2007, p. H16242.

aa. Total FY2009 funding for OAA programs was $2,271.804 million. This includes $2,051.804 million from the FY2009 Omnibus Appropriations Act (P.L. 111-8) and $220.000 million from ARRA.

bb. Formerly known as Alzheimer's Disease Demonstration Grants to the States. The FY1999 Omnibus Consolidated Appropriations Act (P.L. 105-277) transferred the administration of the program from the Health Resources and Services Administration (HRSA) to the AOA. The program is authorized under Secs. 398 and 398B of the Public Health Service Act (42 U.S.C. §§280c-3 to 280c-5). Appropriations were authorized from FY1988 through FY2002.

cc. P.L. 106-501 required the President to convene the conference no later than December 31, 2005. It was held December 11-14, 2005. See http://www.whcoa.gov. FY2006 obligations for the White House Conference on Aging were funded by carryover balances of prior-year appropriations.

dd. The Lifespan Respite Care program is authorized by Title XXIX of the Public Health Service Act (PHSA, 42 U.S.C. §§300ii to 300ii-4). Appropriations were authorized from FY2007 through FY2011.

ee. Health Care Fraud and Abuse Control (HCFAC) funds have historically been provided to the Senior Medicare Patrol Program. HCFAC Funds are distributed to anti-fraud activities from the Medicare Trust Fund at the joint discretion of the HHS Secretary and Attorney General. In addition, the Senior Medicare Patrol program receives funding under OAA Title II: $9.420 million in FY2011 and $9.402 million in FY2012.

ff. Sec. 2405 of the Patient Protection and Affordable Care Act (ACA, P.L. 111-148, as amended) provided mandatory appropriations for ADRCs of $10.0 million for each year from FY2010 to FY2014. In addition, ADRCs receive funding under Title II: $16.469 million obligated in FY2010 under Aging Network Support Activities, $6.469 million in FY2011, and $6.469 million in FY2012.

gg. For Chronic Disease Self-Management Programs (CDSMPs), FY2012 funds were provided under the authority of PHSA Sec. 311 (42 U.S.C. §243, on general authority for cooperation), PHSA Sec. 317(k)(2) (42 U.S.C. §247b(k)(2) on preventive health services project grants), and ACA Sec. 4002 (42 U.S.C. §300u-11, on the Prevention and Public Health Fund, PPHF). For more information about the PPHF see Appendix B in CRS Report R41737, *Public Health Service (PHS) Agencies: Overview and Funding, FY2010-FY2012*, coordinated by C. Stephen Redhead and Pamela W. Smith; and the CRS memorandum *Overview of the Prevention and Public Health Fund (PPHF)*, by Sarah Lister (available by request). In FY2010, AOA received $32.500 million in ARRA funds for CDSMPs, for use in FY2010 and FY2011. These funds were transferred to AOA from $650 million that ARRA had provided to HHS for evidence-based prevention and wellness programs.

hh. The National Clearinghouse for Long-Term Care Information was established by the Deficit Reduction Act of 2005 (DRA), P.L. 109-171, Sec. 6021(d), which appropriated $3.000 million each year for FY2006 through FY2010. ACA Sec. 8002(d) extended the funding, at the same level, through FY2015. Funding in FY2011 to administer the Clearinghouse was via a reimbursable agreement from CMS to AOA. FY2012 funding is provided directly to AOA for program administration. The American Taxpayer Relief Act of 2012 (ATRA, P.L. 112-240) had the effect of canceling the Clearinghouse funding for FY2014 and FY2015, and rescinding any unobligated balances of Clearinghouse funds for FY2013.

ii. Per personal communication with the HHS Budget Office, HHS plans to transfer funds to AOA from the PPHF to carry out certain goals of the National Plan to Address Alzheimer's Disease. Under this plan, AOA would receive $4 million in FY2012 and $4.2 million in FY2013 for education and outreach to enhance public awareness of Alzheimer's disease. AOA would also receive $10.5 million in FY2013 to expand supports for people with Alzheimer's disease and their caregivers in the community.

jj. In FY2012, $6.0 million was transferred to AOA from PPHF to pilot test interventions to prevent elder abuse, neglect, and exploitation. HHS, Prevention and Public Health Fund, FY 2012 Allocation of Funds, http://www.hhs.gov/open/recordsandreports/prevention/index.html; HHS, "HHS grants to help protect seniors, test elder abuse prevention strategies," press release, June 14, 2012, http://www.hhs.gov/news/press/2012pres/06/20120614a.html; AOA, PPHF – 2012 – Elder Abuse Prevention Interventions Program: Program Announcement and Grant Application Instructions, OMB Approval No. 0985-0018, 2012, http://aoa.gov/Grants/Funding/docs/2012/FY2012_PA_EA_Prevention_Final_508.pdf; AOA, "Protecting America's Seniors: The Elder Abuse Prevention Interventions Program," press release, November 1, 2012, http://aoa.gov/aoaroot/Press_Room/News/2012/ElderAbusePreventionGrants.pdf.

kk. Section 119 of the Medicare Improvements for Patients and Providers Act of 2008 (MIPPA, P.L. 110-275) provided $25 million in FY2009 for outreach and education to those eligible for Medicare low-income assistance programs. Of that amount, $7.5 million was allocated for SHIPs within CMS; the rest was allocated to AOA-administered activities: $7.5 million for AAAs, $5.0 million for ADRCs, and $5.0 million for the National Center for Benefits Outreach and Enrollment.

ll. ACA Section 3306 extended MIPPA Section 119 to provide an additional $45.0 million for Medicare enrollment assistance activities for the period of FY2010 through FY2012. ACA allocated the funds to SHIPs, AAAs, ADRCs, and the National Center for Benefits and Outreach Enrollment in the same proportion as under MIPPA. In FY2010, $15.0 million was sent to CMS for SHIPs, and the rest was transferred to AOA for the other activities: $15.0 million for AAAs, $10.0 million for ADRCs, and $5.0 million for the National Center for Benefits and Outreach Enrollment. No additional funds were provided for these activities in FY2011 or FY2012. The American Taxpayer Relief Act of 2012 (ATRA) extended funding under MIPPA to provide for these activities to FY2013; see "Medicare Enrollment Assistance Activities."

Appendix C. Older Americans Act: Authorization of Appropriations

Table C-1 shows the authorization of appropriations for each title of the act as stipulated by the 2006 Older Americans Act Amendments (P.L. 109-365).

Table C-1. Authorization of Appropriations for Older Americans Act Programs in P.L. 109-365

Older Americans Act Programs	Authorization of Appropriations	OAA Section / U.S. Code Section
Title II, Administration on Aging[a]		
Administration of the Act, Authority of Assistant Secretary	Such sums as may be necessary.	Sec. 205(c) / 42 U.S.C. 3016(c)
Administration on Aging	FY2007-FY2011, such sums as may be necessary.	Sec. 216(a) / 42 U.S.C. 3020f(a)
Eldercare Locator	FY2007-FY2011, such sums as may be necessary.	Sec. 216(b) / 42 U.S.C. 3020f(b)
Pension counseling and information program	FY2007-FY2011, such sums as may be necessary.	Sec. 216(c) / 42 U.S.C. 3020f(c)
Title III, State and Community Programs on Aging		
Supportive services and centers	FY2007-FY2011, such sums as may be necessary.	Sec. 303(a) / 42 U.S.C. 3023(a)
Congregate nutrition services	FY2007-FY2011, such sums as may be necessary.	Sec. 303(b)(1) / 42 U.S.C. 3023(b)(1)
Home-delivered nutrition services	FY2007-FY2011, such sums as may be necessary.	Sec. 303(b)(2) / 42 U.S.C. 3023(b)(2)
Disease prevention and health promotion	FY2007-FY2011, such sums as may be necessary.	Sec. 303(d) / 42 U.S.C. 3023(d)
Family caregiver support	FY2007, $160 million; FY2008, $165.5 million; FY2009, $173 million; FY2010, $180 million; FY2011, $187 million.	Sec. 303(e) / 42 U.S.C. 3023(e)
Nutrition services incentive program	FY2007-FY2011, such sums as may be necessary.	Sec. 311(e) / 42 U.S.C. 3030a(e)
Title IV, Activities for Health, Independence, and Longevity		
	FY2007-FY2011, such sums as may be necessary.	Sec. 411(b) / 42 U.S.C. 3032(b)
Title V, Community Service Senior Opportunities Act		
Community Service Employment for Older Americans	FY2007-FY2011, such sums as may be necessary.	Sec. 517(a) / 42 U.S.C. 3056o(a)

Older Americans Act Programs	Authorization of Appropriations	OAA Section / U.S. Code Section
Title VI, Grants for Native Americans		
Indian and Native Hawaiian programs	FY2007 and subsequent fiscal years, such sums as may be necessary.	Sec. 643(1) / 42 U.S.C. 3057n(1)
Native American caregiver support program	FY2007, $6.5 million; FY2008, $6.8 million; FY2009, $7.2 million; FY2010, $7.5 million; FY2011, $7.9 million.	Sec. 643(2) / 42 U.S.C. 3057n(2)
Title VII, Vulnerable Elder Rights Protection Activities		
Subtitle A—State Programs		
Long-term care ombudsman program	FY2007 and subsequent fiscal years, such sums as may be necessary.	Sec. 702(a) / 42 U.S.C. 3058a(a)
Elder abuse, neglect, and exploitation prevention program	FY2007 and subsequent fiscal years, such sums as may be necessary.	Sec. 702(b) / 42 U.S.C. 3058a(b)
Legal assistance development program	FY2007 and subsequent fiscal years, such sums as may be necessary.	Sec. 702(c) / 42 U.S.C. 3058a(c)
Subtitle B—Native American Organization and Elder Justice Provisions		
Native American elder rights program[b]	FY2007 and subsequent fiscal years, such sums as may be necessary.	Sec. 751(d) / 42 U.S.C. 3058aa(d)
Grants for state elder justice systems[b]	FY2007 and subsequent fiscal years, such sums as may be necessary.	Sec. 751(d) / 42 U.S.C. 3058aa(d)

Source: The Older Americans Act of 1965, P.L. 89-73, as amended. Includes the most recent amendments to the act, under the Older Americans Act Amendments of 2006 (P.L. 109-365).

Notes:

a. Two provisions in the act require the Assistant Secretary to make certain amounts available for certain activities: Sec. 202(a)(18)(B) makes available to the National Long-Term Care Ombudsman Resource Center not less than the amount of resources made available to the National Long-Term Care Ombudsman Resource Center for FY2000. Sec. 202(d)(4) states that the Assistant Secretary shall make available to the National Center on Elder Abuse such resources as are necessary for the Center to carry out effectively the functions of the Center under this act and not less than the amount of resources made available to the Resource Center on Elder Abuse for FY2000.

b. The act authorizes appropriations for Subtitle B, which includes the Native American elder rights program and Grants for state elder justice systems.

Author Contact Information

Angela Napili
Information Research Specialist
anapili@crs.loc.gov, 7-0135

Kirsten J. Colello
Specialist in Health and Aging Policy
kcolello@crs.loc.gov, 7-7839

Acknowledgments

Parts of this report were originally authored by Carol O'Shaughnessy. The graphics were created by Jamie Hutchinson.